First edition
10 9 8 7 6 5 4 3 2 1

Library of Congress Control Number: 2019919271
ISBN: 978-1-7343364-1-2

Edited by Stephanie Rodarte
Design by Mark Pearsall

Set in Garamond

www.alifeconcussed.com

A LIFE CONCUSSED

A MEMORIAM OF BRAIN INJURY, ADDICTION & HOMELESSNESS

JEFF GOULD

DEDICATION

THIS BOOK IS DEDICATED TO RICK RYPIEN, A HERO OF
MINE, AND TO ALL THOSE WHO HIT THEIR HEAD, HAD THEIR
LIVES CHANGED FOREVER; AND TO ALL THOSE, WHO WERE NEVER
RECLAIMED TO TELL THE TALE.

ACKNOWLEDGMENTS

I would like to thank Marie Krebs, who planted a seed that was to sprout and grow over the course of many mornings in the spring; I would like to thank Stephanie Rodarte, my editor who instilled in me great confidence when I'd falter, and I was happy to return the favor. Her talent and abilities carved something wonderful out of stone. I would like to thank Mark Miller and Obie Hindman whose words of encouragement spanning back decades always gave me the will to keep trying. My oldest living childhood friend — Jeremy Gypton, for re-accepting an olive branch of friendship after years of my derelictions, and who was present when both concussions took place. I'd like to thank Dr Jon Cavanaugh for teaching me a bit about brain science and supporting my work here. I'd like to thank friends far and near in the hockey community, the musical community; And, of course, my family, who patience, forgiveness, and hardlines were necessary to provoke a birth into an entirely new life. And to my lovely wife Hilary O'hara, I love you very much and now, you know the whole story.

CONTENTS

FORWORD

What a magnificent tool we have been given — this thinking mind. It can learn to say goodnight in ten different dialects, memorize patterns of notes that turn into majestic symphonies, solve complex mathematical equations that result in exploring a mile deep trek into the ocean, or jettison us up high above the planet staring down in orbit; it can even pick through its own history — as I have done here — recollecting details carefully and synchronizing them into a book.

I have spent a good few years now working in crisis intervention, with another decade predating that working in the field of behavioral health. I have always told families that is a natural inclination of human beings to 'bounce back' from ill health, as if genetically programmed into our wiring. Things like white blood cells attacking a foreign bacterial host, bones healing themselves is in our genes, our cells, our thoughts, to cling to life until the final moment when life slips away. Of course, when it comes to *the brain itself,* based on personal experience, I would have to say that it does not so much work *through* things as it learns to work *around* them.

I read a study a while back in regard to attachment disorders. It stated something to the effect of young infants that are held often — in the course of that contact — produce a chemical release that comes from human touch which forms the brain creases and development, all on its own accord. Simply put, the act of being nursed, of being held, of being kept warm nurtures mental growth. In the face of being deprived of that altogether — like so many I have worked with over the years who were adopted from Russian orphanages, devoid of any attention whatsoever, let alone physical touch — the results are disastrous. Malformed from the start, these cases turn into nasty personality disorders wherein the sufferer is as likely to set a garbage can on fire for attention as they are to take out to trash for affirmation. In some cases, their ability to recover from that condition, in the terms of a return to a state of good wholesome living, is well beyond their mental capacity.

Other events which cause mental disorders could range from a colossal and unexpected disappointment to seeing a person die in a car accident, and certainly the highly intense duties of combat can produce an emotion so strong the corpus callosum cannot process it through both hemispheres of the brain, and a condition called 'complex trauma' results, where the dark and disturbing event literally becomes trapped in the central nervous system with a wide scattering of symptoms indicating the past is a constant issue.

Other conditions, compulsive disorders of every type, are merely short bursts of pleasure-seeking stimuli generated by the basal ganglia which has become unharnessed from the frontal parts of the lobes that weigh out things like logic and consequence.

All these cases — simply put — are experience(s) guiding experience, to which we naturally adapt and try to function through — or rather, around — our own limitations. I have a good deal of experience with this.

Then, of course, a sharp blow to the head — a baseball, a hockey puck, a perfect connection from a boxing glove, a door off the hinges knocking someone square in the face, or being knocked unconscious — can bruise, can chaotically disorganize, can readjust this fragile and beautiful instrument altogether. The signs and symptoms of CTE, chronic traumatic encephalopathy, are vastly inconclusive due to diagnosis only occurring postmortem. What science does tell us is that there is, in fact, an effect — potentially grave in nature — to receiving any type of concussive force.

Let me say I am not a doctor, nor a neurologist — far from it. That said, I do love hard science; I appreciate medical journals filled with complex data, and yet, I have always found the statement to be true: truth is stranger than fiction.

What I hope to convey to the reader is not from a scientific perspective but a human perspective, with decades of painful struggle, and dare I say, a changed personality that came from a nasty blow to the head. I hope it serves as a beacon of hope that we all can change, and we all can get well.

—Jeff

PROLOGUE

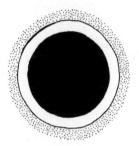

I will tell you, I am skeptical of most things, and when approaching new information, I come in generally guarded if not in an outright cynical way. Most of the therapeutic science in the latter part of the book was greeted with a healthy pessimism when it first presented itself; I have, since, found much of it so vitally important to living a useful life. Conversely, to face one's own shadow unassisted, to go into one's own bone marrow without faith, in my experience, was nearly impossible. Maybe in my more recent years, having come into adulthood from painful experiences, it was choosing to operate out of a new belief system that gave me the courage to ever go into the depths of myself in the first place. In this, I have shared a wealth of experience around particular things I have found invaluable.

From an earlier time in my life, my only sort of spiritual 'beliefs' were a maze of superstitions interwoven with a genuine belief that I might very well have been the unluckiest person on the planet. Two decades ago, I met up with a woman who claimed to have some gifts of foresight and hindsight. She named off a handful of events that proved to be frighteningly accurate. Like I stated before, in listening to her claims, I was extremely skeptical, yet curious. I played along, if for no other reason than to tactfully discredit her psychic gifts. I remember her telling me, "You've had a terrible head injury as a boy, and it changed who you were. It changed the way you thought, and the way you felt."

Let me say this: I do not have a speech impediment, nor do I have any noticeable facial scarring from having been concussed severely not once but twice. It might have been a lucky guess, but other facts about my life that were laid out plainly, led me to believe that something more than manipulation happened that day. She was right, that grey three-pound globe of flesh had been jarred, altered ever so slightly, opening up things in my world I never wished to see, and perhaps to some degree, placing my feet on a path to places I never imagined I would go. I would never guess the concussive significance, nor the inspiration that would later come of it.

In undertaking this work, let me add this is not a testimony to victimhood — nobody loves a victim — nor is this lobbing the improbable theory that a simple head injury was one hundred percent the culprit for all the trouble I faced, which was incredulous. Looking back, I know there were many reasons for what amounted to an extended period of homelessness, for an insatiable need to be blindly intoxicated with poor decision making, certainly not the least of them. I liken my situation to that of an insurance adjuster evaluating a car wreck where, from the crash, a percentage of blame is assigned to the operator and a percentage to road conditions or weather. A scattered field of family members have had their own bouts with alcohol, though most, if not all, were living very successfully, well-adjusted lives. For me, this simply was not the case. To see the disparity of their academic achievements and my derelictions, you might not have guessed we were related whatsoever. It is hard to say, for sure, how much impact being concussed actually caused for me.

I have a friend back in Arizona, Leo, who said something along, "sorting ourselves out when we have lived as (sic you) I did, was like untangling a giant ball of yarn." I have found that to be true. I would be highly likely — in any kind of heavy physiological evaluation — to score marks in several categories. In my forty-six years of history as of this writing, I had a wild array of disfunction which included five years of insomnia, a substance abuse disorder, a handful of instances that may very well have put me on a chart as having a personality disorder of some sort, and — this I do not say lightly — paired with a significant trauma history.

I do not wear these as a badge of honor. In fact, I feel neutral about them, if not grateful. Many of these have built a resilience in me, and most importantly, made me effective when working with people with similar trouble. Of course, having said that, all these pieces of my life went largely unevaluated, some or most of the means of treating these was years away from being discovered; I never had the words to describe my interior, not back then. It was a quiet and internal dis-ease that drove me, coupled with dark imaginings that had me question my own sanity from an early age; but it seemed to be the head injury that was the catalyst that changed everything... at least in my world.

You may suffer as I did. You may see a physician that would set you upon a trajectory wildly different from anything you may have read in this book. It may involve taking medications that I have no experience, and thus no opinion. It might involve certain modalities of therapy which, in my experience, have gone untested and that may, very well, bring relief. And, it could be they are right, and I am wrong. This is merely some background of how I not only survived myself, but also acclimated to a world that was once burdensome and full of snares. As a whole, I think medical science is on the precipice of just now *barely* beginning to understand how the mind works, and how to treat head injuries and help this three-pound muscle to heal itself.

That said, this body of work is meant to serve as a beacon of hope to those who have or are struggling with head injury, CTE or TBI symptoms, and who have suffered a collapse in their life as a result. My practices that have helped me to function normally and overcome the greatest of odds are not the 'end all be all.' These new sciences I spoke of, regarding brain science, appear on the horizon, things like trans-magnetic therapy for depression and differing types of neurofeedback.

I am hopeful and encouraged by the sea of practitioners, scholars and colleagues who I am fortunate to spend time collaborating with on a regular basis; they have helped me heal and discover layers of truth about myself. Many encouraged, supported and counseled me in writing this body of work. And to the rest, well, there are individuals in this world who have pulled me out of the furthest reaches of the abyss, to whom I owe my life.

THE HAPPIEST DAYS OF OUR LIVES

Suzanne, my mom, was born in St. Louis in 1938. Her dad, Ron, Sr., was a devout Catholic while his wife, Suzanne Wolfe, always wrestled a bit with his religious values and adhering to them. I know so little about this part of my mom's life, other than Grandma had her friends at the bar and had to be put out of the house now and again because of her drinking, which she would attempt to curtail in the interest of keeping the family together. One time I know of, she had abandoned her marriage for three months, seeking out the nightlife, drawn to bottles and socialization, before she would come limping back — remorseful and apologetic — to resume being a parent and a housewife.

She had her pride and her vanities, one of which was making a 'sound' judgement that my mom, when she was a kid, had feet that were too big and unbecoming for a young woman. As a result, my mom has deformed feet to this day from wearing shoes two sizes too small as a young kid.

My mother's quiet demeanor, which was matched with my own either lack of interest or isolated self-involvement left much of her early years — her likes and dislikes — an utter mystery to me. I know only bits and pieces of my mother's story. This may prove to be something I might forever regret, never having taken a deep interest in my family and the things that mattered to them.

Looking back, we were raised with church and its core values. We were given education — at least the opportunity for it — but sometimes what appears to be a loving web of inter-connectedness that I have seen in family-life of friends growing up — families that Christmas caroled together or took goofy family photos — was, perhaps, absent. We were each an island unto ourselves in many ways, though the trappings of family-life were there, from the outside looking in.

My mom joined the Air Force to get into nursing, following her brother Ron, Jr. on a path that my grandmother was never in agreement. Through her vodka filled days and some heavy mannerisms, Grandma Wolfe doted on her son, Ron, who she feared his leaving home, to which she was equally sensitive and terror-stricken by lightning storms; these things I know to be true. Grandma was hard on the women in her life, probably as younger women see other women as threating, perhaps even competition. My mom and my sister, Kris, both took the brunt of that, but she was, simply, who she was.

Mom enjoyed her time in nursing school in Germany and told me, once, how she liked to ride in the back of hotshot fighter pilots on weekends off, when she was looking for a kick. That was always hard for me to picture: my mom getting a drink or two in her and sauntering down the runway looking to fly with some jockey she had never met before. I suspect these were probably her best days, or some of them.

She met my dad, Karl, overseas and would tell me much later in life that he was the man she lost her virginity to, and that was in her thirties — one of those facts you would just assume to not know altogether. My mom was a good, Catholic square like that, had always been put off by Grandma's habits of men and liquor, and chose for herself a different path.

Dad, in his younger years, had run marathons, had an intense wit and good humor, and seemed like a good suitor, so, naturally, they were engaged shortly after meeting. The wedding plans were doused by one sad reality. That same year, 1969, Ron, Jr. would crash his Navy jet into a small island in the Pacific where he was killed instantly, something that peaked my interest because my mom and I shared — in depth — so rarely but she confided something that had happened a year or two after that event.

After the accident and the standards of the Military to bring the folded flag home, Grandma had a severe, mental breakdown filled with an anguish that I suspect she never quite recovered. This would drive her to skip her daughter's, my mother's, wedding altogether, claiming it was 'too soon' and the family ought remain in mourning.

Suzanne and Karl were married for five years. Much of that time, we lived in townhouses around Torrance and Manhattan Beach that I remember little of as my parent's relationship deteriorated. Dad had always had a quick temper with all his spouses (and there have been several), and was equally hard and impatient with his small children. Though she would, later, downplay the divorce for lots of reasons, I think dad being as heavy-handed as he was on his kids, brought up a deep, maternal need in mom's world to get her children as far away from his blusterous, wild explosions that were beginning to become a frequent occurrence; some of our spankings and discipline in those early years seemed to occur without restraint, and what was meant to be a few, well-placed swats often turned into a violent and terrifying thrashing.

I know from some brief family talks that, back then, we would move around a little near the hospital my mom had taken to working several shifts a week. I can visualize patches of strawberries grown in thick bunches from a thicket around the corner from one home; I remember that. I, also, remember having a silver car that I liked to play with. In fact, I remember falling down the stairs once; I remember a swim lesson that took place at the hands of my father that felt like a near drowning. I have very few memories of those years like most adults pondering something decades past. *The spotty fragments of memories from just a few rotations around the sun are interesting things to ponder.*

It was 4:30AM when we left Los Angeles. I was five years old, my sister a year and a half older. My mom had tearfully written out a two-page goodbye letter and tucked it neatly under a placemat on the kitchen table where she knew my dad — then away on business — would find it. Our departure followed what had been the latest in a series of nasty, marital battles that had increased in both volume and collateral damage. This one was particularly loud as the china from the cabinet exploded against walls, fragments of plates, saucers and cups engraved with delicate flowers spraying shards of porcelain across the dining room. Kris remembers this well, but for me, it was more abstract, for I was four years old. Only a day or two had passed after that episode before dad was to leave on business; and when he did, we left both my father and sunny Los Angeles for good.

We were packed up in a red Fiat, Kris and I tucked into the back seat with soft, green blankets, a worried looking miniature Sheltie Collie standing guard over her charges. We were on the freeway before the sun had risen, an irritated and miserable Calico stuck in a small wooden and wire box, howling loudly at a sudden change of environment. The cat and dog intermittently took turns evacuating in the car, and mom would pullover on the Interstate 10 and grab them by the scruff before placing them back in the backseat and ferrying on. When the sun started to rise, we may have been driving through that large windmill farm near Palm Springs. We barreled east to the desert where a small but friendly hotel housed us until the paperwork for the final sale of the house had the ink dried, and we piled what we had into that four-bedroom east side home in Tucson. For several days, mom, Kris and I slept in sleeping bags in this great, big sprawl of a house with pizza boxes and milk cartons scattered on the floor. For better or worse, we were home. It was 1977.

At that point, the visits with our older siblings — technically halves — got fewer and further between even though we had always all considered ourselves brothers and sisters. Spencer, over a decade my senior, was a brilliant musician who had left the Navy to enlist for the FBI, which was a dream that had never panned out, and ended up an IRS man instead, sometimes doing seizures of million dollar properties in Manhattan, which made for good story telling. Gina, my eldest sister, was a very scientifically minded PHD who has studied everything from digging up dinosaur bones to botany and everything in between.

That house, as it were, had a brilliant and tactile mark of its era. In the front room was a deep crimson shag carpet, while the rest of the house wielded a wild lime green carpet in the same style. I always loved that, the wild contrast that was put together with prints of Picasso's hung in almost every room. The house was a mosaic of yellows and blues, reds and greens. Years later — when my mother would put in tan ceramic tile and settle for a new coat of paint with the generic and worn earthly tones that all the neighbors had as well, an acceptable and uninventive palate of desert colors with a combination of either tan or turquoise everywhere — I remember having disappointment because I have always loved a wide palate of color, and still very much do today.

We were enrolled in the nearby school, Marshall, which hedged the well-manicured golf course that sprawled out between us and it. I would attend school there for a number of years while a small but steady-growing savings fund was being added to monthly so Kris and I could attend a private, Catholic school several miles west of us; neither she nor I would have a clean ending at that Catholic school, having grown adversarial to the faculty, a group of bitter nuns better suited for slaughtering farm animals than for teaching children, but we were given a fine education.

We had not been in our new home too terribly long before my interest in sports would take hold and I was enlisted to play for an AYSO soccer league; I think I may have been around nine at the time. Having seen what abilities I had, I would be relegated as a right fullback, which even later in life when I took up hockey, would always be hovering in my corner, my duties to retrieve whatever might have been coming back, and make a strong first kick or first pass out of the zone, to turn the direction of the play going the other way. At times, I envied the forwards; I suppose they call them strikers nowadays in the professional leagues, as it appeared the glory was always up front. Even at that time, a half-back would have made a most welcome promotion. But my skillset was never being fleet of foot, with the coordination that a promotion of that sort would certainly require.

Our goalie was this kid Shawn who had a host of medical problems a few years down the road, and who would ultimately expire before ever seeing the age of twenty or so. As I recall, we held practices at both the nearby schoolyard and the field of the nearby seminary where those who had dedicated their life to religion had taken up study. That building — walking near it or around it — always had deep comfort to me. Decades later, I would sit at that same seminary under the lit up statue of the Virgin Mary, beneath a quiet sky full of stars, swooning from intoxication, and pondering my life and the idea to end it abruptly.

Our sponsoring body was a nearby Catholic church, the Church of St. Francis. We met as a team, our coaching staff headed by my friend Kurt's father, Bud. He was kind and gentle and had a good, well-rounded knowledge of the game. Building a soccer club rotted in democracy, he held a clipboard as we all sat Indian-style on the field around him in a semi-circle. "Ok, boys. We're going to throw out some names, and then we are going to take the top three, and vote on them. This is your team, so take pride in it, and let's figure out a name we can all be proud of."

I do not remember any of the suggestions, except I remember — quite clearly — coming up with one of my own. "How about the 'Demons'?" I asked. Bud raised his eyebrows, let out a heavy sigh, and added it to the clipboard. Moments later, a few more were added, while a few duds sparked controversy and were scribbled out with a pencil. And, so, sitting there under the setting sun, we took a vote. And we became the 'St. Francis Demons,' for whom I played defense for four or five years.

I, also, had a knack for swimming, the butterfly being my stroke. Many good memories of clear, desert mornings and being in the pool practicing my stroke. The smell of chlorine in that bright desert air was a welcome one, coupled with the lingering smell of freshly cut grass on the nearby course. Those are the things that stand out to me most about those early years, and as far as memories go, they were the happiest days of our lives.

As far back as I can remember, I was a self-contained and self-involved kid. I was perfectly happy to eat meals on my own, to sit in my bedroom and draw by myself, and much of those early years, I chalked up to being a passenger — rather than a participant — in the nucleus of the family. Even in school, where I tended to excel when I wanted, there was this deadpan vacant space I would fall into, daydreaming in class, tuned into some foreign radio frequency, sitting there with my mouth agape and staring ahead, at nothing at all. "Earth to Astronaut Gould; come in Astronaut Gould," I remember the teacher would joke, before a good bit of laughter would pull me up out from that fog and deposit me back at my folding desk. My dad, for his part, was much the same way; he would often stare off into space and would become inaccessible for long stretches of minutes. He would twist his finger in his hair, staring blankly ahead, and it often took calling his name upwards of five times to get his attention.

My dad was a self-described 'cold-warrior' who, in later years, would do a good bit of engineering work for Titan Missiles and serve as a high-paid independent consultant for those who made weapons and wished to sell them privately to the military. Long after the era of the home computer was in full stride, dad would sit at his drawing table with these giant books of graph paper, penciling perfectly along the lines the make-up circuit boards and wiring harnesses for ICBM missile systems. He stated flat-out that he hated computers, which was nothing new. My dad stated he hated plenty of things.

After the divorce, we traveled one week every summer to see him. The upside was that, even then, I loved to travel, new sights and new smells, things of interest. I had never seen a train up close and personal until he moved to Colorado Springs. Kris, my sister, and I would head out to the tracks almost every day with a handful of pennies, dimes and nickels that we lined up perfectly along the tracks, admiring with awe and wonder the flat and featureless circles of metal that it would give us in return after the train had passed.

Dad had, perhaps, the largest collection of science fiction books anyone had ever seen; his study housed roughly ten bookcases, each reaching nearly the ceiling with hundreds — possibly thousands — of books arranged alphabetically by author. Some were of the outer space variety with illustrated covers of tall spacesuit clad vixens perched up on some sort of lunar rock blasting a slime green alien in the face with a ray gun of some sort, while others were more of the classic swords and sorcery stuff. I spent hours up there, meticulously going from book to book, just to look at the covers. And, even though, over the span of a couple of years, I saw the entire catalog, I would start the project over and go through them one-by-one again.

That said, it was always good to return home from those weeklong summer trips. My dad had a strong personality with an out-of-control temper one would walk on eggshells around, smelling of clamato and vodka and that heavy Benson & Hedges scent that always smelled so inviting; much later on, I would become a smoker myself.

And so, those early forming years went like that: long, hot summer days in the desert on the far eastside of Tucson, the nearby desert brush disappearing year after year as development took over, swimming in the summers, soccer through the school year, and hating every bit of our private school education, though I know it served us well.

Mom got me involved with the scouts when I was seven or eight. Here I was, this self-involved daydreaming kid who would walk around panting with his mouth wide open, tying knots and trying to earn merit badges; these were things, at that time, that did not make a lot of sense to me, and I certainly had little ambition around it. I did not look at those troop meetings as particularly friendly, nor as something to immerse myself. They were — if anything — a distraction from after school kid's television programming one day a week, which was a staple of such days. There was, though, a light at the end of that scout-tunnel which did very much interest and excite me. At the end of the school year, the scout troop had a derby race wherein each kid was to be given the same materials: a block of balsa wood, some plastic wheels, a few lead weights, and several weeks to build his derby car, which would, then, compete in a series of time trails until a winner prevailed from among them.

That project immediately overtook my interest. I, again, pulled out that loose-leaf notebook and began making plans, which I would scribble out almost daily before revising them to a much more winning effort. *Did I want flames, or racing stripes, and what would be a lucky number to pick?* These things filled my imagination with wonder and possibility as time crept towards the day of that big race.

I watched in awe and amazement as the other scouts, over a period of weeks, brought their carved balsa wood cars to school in their backpacks, presumably to show them off. Some were painted bright red, others a flat black; some were shaped like an arrow, with the wheels extending out widely past the chassis, others were more complex, like a sculpted version of a Camaro with lots of contour. I would ask to look at each one; turning it carefully over in my hands, admiring its qualities and the skill it took to build it.

I began rummaging around in mom's junk drawer where I found a hammer, a Phillips-head screwdriver, an old door hinge, and some sealing caulk, now dried up and nasty in the tube. I found an old butter knife and tried to saw away, carving gentle curves into the wood, but to no avail; that simply was not going to work, no matter what I tried. For reasoning I do not know, it **never** occurred to me to ask for help.

I sat there, on my bed, looking at the cartoonish calendar my mom had hung for me, to keep track of things. Every day prior to that scout derby race had been absently marked off with a giant 'x' to count down the days until the event, which now, became today.

I sat there, blinking, staring at the block of wood sitting on my desk, the wheels still crisp in a plastic package, the numbered stickers splayed across the desk's surface. The time had come, then gone, to build my little car. The rest of the kids were somewhere up the street, standing alongside proud fathers, cheering and applauding this race. But I would not race today, nor did I wish to attend. In fact, all I really wanted was to vanish. It felt like a stunning defeat.

LIGHTS OUT

Brady skated out onto the sheet of smooth ice, his sharp skates getting traction, and he took his three powerful strides as the rest of his team — tough and gritty — followed him out of the tunnel, some with blackened eyes or pulled ligaments, dropping their sticks to the ice, swirling in rotation and eyeing the home team, the Cornwall Aces, who, too, came to play.

The crows of several thousand in this province of Ontario were on their feet intermittently, cheering for the big play, screaming at phantom penalties that went uncalled, creating chants to energize the home team.

Brady scored a goal in the first part of the third period: a slick shot off the wrist that had beaten the goalie glove-side. He was drafted by Montreal, one hundred forty-ninth overall, this storied franchise with its French speaking coaches and case full of trophies going back a hundred years. So, out of high school, with high ambition but still the frailty of any teenager leaving home, he packed a large duffel bag, his skates, pads and helmet in a separate and far fouler smelling bag, said goodbye to his parents, and headed up to eastern Canada on his own.

This night, the crowd seemed vibrant and alive, a living mass of cheers and heckling, arms raised, the masses gathered to cheer for their gladiator players, all with a singular aspiration: to make it to the big show. His seven previous concussions were the last thing on his mind; he felt strong and confident in his skates, his skill and compete level fully on display.

His arms felt cool; his thoughts composed; a flood of what might have been pride, if not cocksureness, gave him a boost as he glided back to the bench with warm congrats and high fives from his friends, a soft pat of the shoulder from the coach.

Doug Friedman, who Brady played against when he was playing college hockey in Providence, skated out with Brady's line. Having already played the better part of three periods in a well-rounded game, just a short time after puck drop, Brady obliged Doug by dropping the gloves and a short taunt. Doug gave him the nod, and his gloves came off; a flurry of fists went crosswise, and Brady lost his footing in the process. The seconds stretched timelessly as both Brady's confidence and delivery drained out of him; the sharp crack of fists raining down on his helmet. The blur of the arena lights, the roar of the crowd, and the jarring punches repeatedly striking him seemed to break something loose. And what it was would cast the end of his all-too-short career.

The next day, the anxiety and depression were overwhelming, a curtain of grey that swallowed Brady whole, in the belly of a hellish torment. His coaching staff noticed quickly the change altogether in deportment, but the damage was done. The last strands of neural freeways that promoted mental hygiene were damaged and cluttered, and Brady began to sink. Things took on a slow and gutting tone. His brain, now changed, would spiral out of control in a way in which it would take decades to fully recover. A psychiatrist employed by the team had set up a session just days later, as the club figured out their prized prospect was drowning in the mire, but the psychiatrist was given a pat answer, as was the club: "I quit. I don't wish to do this anymore." And the darkness ate him alive.

****

There were a scattered handful of kids throughout our neighborhood whom I would spend time with as a kid. There was Allen, whose mom was Polynesian, and with whom I would spend hours in the afternoon sparring wearing boxing gloves; sometimes, after a prolonged bout, one or the other of us would get pretty upset and have those tears of frustration well up, and really go aggressively at the other, striking wildly before we would end up cancelling our afternoon, only to re-group the following weekend for a rematch. There was David, who lived a bit too far away to ride my bicycle to his mom's house, but whom I loved to visit when my mom had time to drop me off, as he was the first guy I ever met who had a home video gaming system, which was prehistoric by any standard: a series of blips and dots moving through mazes that required a rich imagination to make of some entertainment.

Then, there was Michael, the slender kid with the unkempt brown hair with a decent gap between his two front teeth; mentioning him gives me pause when I think of him today. When we were a bit younger, both of us around seven years of age, the kids with whom we spent time only extended, really, as far as the end of our neighborhood street which stretched north about twenty houses before curving east with a bunch more around the corner. Michael lived around the corner on the curve; hence, I never saw a great deal of him, except on Saturdays at the Rolling Hills pool where he was a familiar face. We splashed each other, as kids do, and talked a little in those days, simple stuff, Marco Polo type of stuff but looking back, I guess I never knew him well, though I did know him.

I have some amount of recollection of getting up one Sunday morning and going to the kitchen where, sometimes (but not always), mom would make homemade doughnuts and leave those out for us with some orange juice when she went to play a round

31

of golf. So, it was with shock and disbelief, when I saw Michael — Michael Perry was his name — on the front page of the Sunday paper pasted with a picture of an older Hispanic guy with a flat expression in mugshot form. Michael had been kidnapped with another kid about his age when leaving a chess tournament in downtown Tucson. They were held captive for two days, abused repeatedly during that time; a daring attempt by one of them to fight back with a shower rod was thwarted, and both were taken to the desert where Michael was tied to a tree and stabbed repeatedly; he died there that day, reportedly screaming for his mother. The survivor, Joel, made his escape through the desert — as the story went — before finding some off-road enthusiasts, who in disbelief of his story, called the police. William Castaneda was arrested that morning, his truck stuck in the sand trying to escape — I think — the end and horrific results of his own nature.

What sticks out to me about that, that whole situation, is how little we spoke of it at home. The things that would make up a person's worst nightmare having become all-too-real, and yet, from what I remember, it was never discussed. Maybe mom did not know what to say, nor what to think...

Then, of course, there was Jeremy, with whom I shared wild imagination; most of our talks revolved around swords, sorcery or our recent discovery of the love of rock and roll music, like Cheap Trick. His family lived but two holes on the golf course away, and for some years, we were inseparable.

We oiled the chains of our bikes — a pit crew in training — taking this task of maintenance and precision far too seriously, though our young years are not so far removed from putting baseball cards in the spokes, at ten years old, Jeremy and I, spending this blur of scorching summer days in the desert outside. For a time, we tried to turn the house dog — a collie — into a racing hound fit for a dog track, she tried to keep up in that friendly nature that all dogs have, but certainly was glad for respite when we tired of that game. We, also, spent countless hours taking in the spray-painted hieroglyphs on a nearby concrete wall — crude and lust filled teenage renditions of sexual acts drawn carefully, or not so carefully. They taught us everything we needed to know about turning fifteen, and what, perhaps, to expect when we got there. But our favorite thing — the absolute best — was the dirt track we helped bring into fruition with an older kid, Earl.

Earl was fourteen, a few years older than either of us, and wore horn rimmed glasses and cowboy boots, and always had a big lip full of chewing tobacco. In fact, he had a pyramid made of it in his bedroom, Copenhagen cans that is. We spent an entire month, four or five of us, building this dirt track through a small arroyo that wrapped around the perimeter of the local school we lived near. For weeks, we labored with shovels and rakes creating a crisscrossing path through this wash of dirt and sand, a most impressive feat for a group of local kids with little else but the expense of time those three-month-long summers offered. It was put to good use by us neighborhood kids.

This day, we rode the track for a little while, stopped for water, and then, headed for the schoolyard. We rode in wide arcs through the schoolyard, the same elementary school that would contain me nine months out of the year where I was perennially dissatisfied and made grades despite a near absence of any cognition whatsoever while there. I was always a kid with a wild imagination, prone to daydreams and higher thinking, while chained to the precepts of being young — like basic arithmetic and learning to write out my name in cursive. We sped around — laughing and cracking jokes — before settling in under the shade of a tree near some picnic tables. "Do you think I should jump this?" I said, eyeing the table.

"I don't think you can," Jeremy said, challenging me.

"Oh, I know I can," I said. *Challenge accepted.*

I lugged my bright, orange bike on top of the table, and climbed up the wooden adjoining bench, mounting the bike which was pointed lengthwise down the end of the picnic table. For some reason, I felt abnormally high up, sitting on top of my bike on top of this table. I felt my palms go clammy and my heart begin to race; a thrilling idea was turning — perhaps — into a bad one, and the plague of self-doubt was consuming as I stared down my six feet of runway at the three-foot drop at the end.

"Ok…. go!" Jeremy chirped.

*I thrust forward a few inches, my right leg on the top pedal, ready to push off … before stopping. My heart is racing fast; it certainly had not looked **this** high before climbing up here. I sit, heart still racing, just two feet from the ledge. I back up my bicycle, again, sizing up the drop.*

"You can do it!" Jeremy said, laughing. *I close my eyes and push forward: three full strokes of the pedal — a meek jerk! The front end of my bike tumbles forward, the horizon of dirt and dried grass racing toward my face, the sensation of tumbling before the dull crack, the deafening blunt shock of bone hitting earth. Black.*

I come to, bewildered. I am alone… only to find out later, my friend has gone to get help. The sun seems bright and dirt and grass are stuck to my face. A dull orb of memory glows, distantly, cutting through the confusion and a head full of what felt like crushed bricks. Jeremy arrives with his mom; they ask — repeatedly — if I am okay, which I assure them, I am, brushing the dirt from my face. Hot pinchers poke at something deep inside my head, and what feels like a thick syrup oozes around behind the features of my face. My thoughts turn to oatmeal, and I wince as trains roar through my head… I tell no one that I have headaches for weeks.

****

It was an impossibly hot summer the next year; looking back, temperatures were enough to fry an egg on the sidewalk, at least that was the type of whimsy you might see on the local 5 o'clock news which would demonstrate such things for the viewers. As such, Jeremy and I would spend more time indoors than out, listening to Iron Maiden records, playing with his junior magic set, drawing pictures, playing cards. His mother would often prompt us to get more exercise, but in one-hundred-and-fourteen degrees, those outings were often short lived.

That summer, his family had taken to do some re-modeling of their low slung but comfortable suburban home: a fresh coat of paint over everything with its heavy vinyl and mildly aromatic paint scent, along with door trim and baseboards. Plastic tarps and used paint brushes and spent rollers, old pieces of trim lay scattered around his house as his two older brothers donned overalls and took to task rolling out a fresh coat of white, more similar than not to the last coat of white.

In the middle of all that, I was sprawled on the floor with a comic book, which — looking back — seems odd: I never much could digest comics, could never make the animated drawings and corresponding story make sense, a bit like watching a bad lip synched movie to me. It just never was my thing.

I remember only a little bit from that day though, to tell the truth.

His brothers are painting. Doors have been taken from their hinges, resting upright against the wall. There are plastic tarps on the ground. I am in the center of the room, laying down, reading.

Jeremy's older brother, Joe, walks in the room carrying a paint roller, brush, and flimsy metal tray. The heavy acrid scent of latex paint fills my nostrils. (I always loved paint and model glue — heavy industrial smells — even as a kid.)

He kicks his way through a wadded-up piece of tarp and sets himself up to take to task the wall in front of him. Jeremy ducks past him. (Well, it might have been Jeremy; it might have been his brother.) An elbow or knee contacts the closet door resting against the wall — freed from its hinges and duties both — until the job gets done.

The door goes upright for a moment before falling backwards like a toppling tower with only myself in its path as it swings in a downward arc. Jeremy shouts for me to look out! (I remember that.)

The sound jolts me, and I turn my head — a fraction of a second in time — before a wooden corner comes swinging wildly down, and a blur of flickering light punches though my reality, tunneling me into the black of space.

I'm aware... vaguely... voices chattering. Flickering points of light dance and tremors of sharp pain shoots from my head to every limb — a bright pitchfork of sensory overload.

I am staring down. I see a white.... surface. A white surface. I collect and come to, staring at what is a red dot; it grows and grows and grows, now, a red globe, expanding and twisting in size with several white stick-like things scattered through the field.

I remember thinking clearly, "Someone spilled an ashtray in front of me," with the white crushed cigarette butts flung wildly about — the white kind, usually associated with a light cigarette. (In the fog, I didn't ponder what sense that did or did not knowing that nobody here was a smoker or had been.)

*My eyesight falls back into focus, and I notice, these are **not** cigarette butts I'm staring at, but upwards of twelve whole teeth: their roots pointy and extended like small tusks. The pool of blood is, now, two feet across and growing, spreading across that plush white carpet, and the only thing I can think to do in this moment is apologize. "I'm sorry. I'm sorry —" I say and begin trying to swallow the blood flowing so wildly and freely from dozens of vacancies. The rich iron taste washes down my throat like a fountain as I swallow mouthful after mouthful. But my stomach rejects this, and next I know, I am projectile vomiting bright, red blood everywhere. Towels are wrapped around my face and mouth. Jeremy can't stop crying. His mom springs into action, and I hear sirens in the background.*

I trace my tongue around a very much unfamiliar territory: what was, once, a familiar and lifelong cavern of clean, white teeth is, now, a malformed and foreign landscape. My gum line is folded neatly up against the roof of my mouth facing east, and my lips balloon out into some nightmarish helium form. A deep and profound sensory mix of swirling thoughts make me dizzy. I hope I wake up from whatever this is, and soon.

I was admitted to St. Joseph's Hospital on that sunny Sunday afternoon, accompanied by only one other patient: a tall and sinewy rough looking character with cowboy boots and a big belt buckle with chunks of — what I later overheard to be — beer bottle embedded tightly in his face. He cussed and roared, flat out stating he was nearly ready to whoop some guy when he was suckered from behind. I stared over at him, a twelve-year-old kid covered in bloody towels, at this afternoon brawler. A nurse pulled a blue sheet separating me from his sight, but not his sounds. His sultry monologue continued for some time.

I sat for upward of three hours; I recall overhearing a surgeon who was on-call was headed in, his eighteen holes of golf quickly cancelled that afternoon for hospital duty, his charge: a bloody heap of a gangly kid, sitting in worry about what would happen next.

My good friend Jeremy, or perhaps it was his mother, had enough foresight to gather the teeth that was cast about on their carpet, and place it in a jelly jar that was passed off to the paramedics en route to the hospital. I remember about a dozen or so Novocain shots, which numbed out the pain, but not the horror of what felt like a pair of medical pliers maneuvering my gums, so they went southward, again.

The long, ivory-like teeth were shoved back into their angry sockets, in some sort of daft reunion, and a wire harness held everything tightly in place. A network of black sutures created rail tracks through both the inside and outside of my mouth and having a nurse for a mother ensured things were always well looked after, and fresh ice packs were always there. Because kids are cruel by nature — their empathic minds still barely formed — my return to class at Catholic school was met with an awkward and cool distance before hours in, some jokes started to circulate, which I nonchalantly brushed off.

****

I notice, looking back at old photo albums full of polaroid's of long forgotten birthday parties with melting chocolate cakes and paper hats, corny noisemakers and confetti strewn about, that from about the age ten on, I always appear to be squinting. I remember eating those small, pink, baby aspirin — sometimes on a daily basis — certainly to numb the pain in my jaw, but most for pounding and catastrophic headaches that would come and go in the most transient of ways, and the light back then... well, it always seemed too bright.

****

It was some months later at twelve, the wire harness was discarded by a friendly orthodontist who would poke and pry, busily wiggling teeth as he stared into my mouth agape with a small penlight inspecting the neat handiwork of his predecessor.

"Things are looking good in there; this came out really nice." Nice seemed like an odd term to describe it, but I always had — since I was much younger — a significant gap in my front teeth, which, now, had been reshaped to my front two teeth being packed tightly together. The headaches continued, as did the almost morbid vampiric disdain for direct sunlight. It came and it went, like almost everything else.

Some months later, I developed what appeared to be a dull throbbing pain that racked my mouth, which in about the span of a week had amplified to a stuttering keel over pain. The tiny nerve-endings in my teeth, nearly distraught and destroyed, were rewiring themselves to my brain, most unpleased. Within a matter of days, every footstep I took felt fresh and bright, like a punch in the face. Not wanting to appear weak, I fought back tears at the pain in my skull, now, totally inescapable.

I called my mother from the nurses' office, and told her what was going on, how bad it all felt. It was maybe 9:00 am that morning, the day still opening up of possibility. I sat there in that dusty nurses' station, inhaling that smell that all old, Catholic schools must have smelt like: stale cleansers, moth balls and aged wood.

Unbeknownst to me, she had phoned the dentist who had anticipated all along the possibility of those nerves one day waking up, angry and punishing upon their return.

"Bring him in now," he said. "The office is free, and we'll just pull the roots from all of them." I was sitting there when my mom returned the call to the school nurse who told me point blank, "Your mom is coming to pick you up. They are bringing you in for thirteen root canals... here, in about an hour." The thought of that, those words, 'root canal,' and knowing there were thirteen of them coming, brought no relief at all. In fact, I would have run down the hallway and escaped, but the pain was so fierce, I could barely walk at all without the vibration pummeling me. Thirteen root canals are exactly what I got. The stitches, and pains in my mouth went away... But the headaches lasted much longer.

NO BEAST SO FIERCE PT I

I have had a friend, Ken, for the past fifteen years or so —
somewhat of a mentor to me in a number of areas of life — who
has championed me, along with many others, in finding lasting
sobriety over the years which was difficult for me, of which I have
not mentioned much. Alcohol had always had a strong pull on me,
like a riptide pulling me out to sea in a hidden current. Ken had
been an iron worker, his lean and sinewy frame wearing a welding
hood, working at his shop in his back yard, cutting and shaping
steel, creating majestic spires of welded artwork for those who had
commissioned him to do so.

Ken was as steady and even keeled as they come; in retrospect,
I do no recall ever hearing him speak ill of another human being.
He radiated — and still does today — warmth and compassion
I have known but only a few to possess. He was focused and
dedicated to be an ironworker, and created a wealth of artwork
that has been sold all over the country.

Unbeknownst to me — and it was only recently that I found
out — Ken had something of a seizure history. I did not sense

from our conversation it is something that happened with any frequency, but every couple of years or so, he would go through a spell where he would have one or two of them. This had been the case in 2018 when he had a seizure at his workbench, fell backward off a chair and concussed his head on the ground.

I heard from a mutual friend Brian about a year prior to this writing that Ken was not feeling well; he was having — what sounded like — visions, perhaps hallucinations, and that he was in a pretty dark spot.

I tend not to invite myself into people's personal struggles or battles, save for when I am asked formally to do so; hence, it was not until I called Ken for a completely different reason, several months later, that it came up as a topic of conversation. I made mention to him that Brian told me he was struggling a bit, though I admit, I was unprepared on any level for his answer, and where that answer might take me.

Ken told me, yes, he had fallen and hit his head. Yes, he had been diagnosed with a concussion. But it is what he said after that that I found... curious.

Ken told me, he frequently had bouts where he pictured — with extreme vividness — his bones snapping wildly and poking out of his skin; he spoke of how he pictured thick, red blood pouring out his ears, how these thoughts would become so overwhelming that they interfered with his ability to work. Sometimes, he would have to lie down, or at other times, maybe go for a walk. Sometimes, these things stayed a while, their toxic effect making him question his sanity; sometimes, they dissipated rather quickly. He told me a few trips to medical professionals had not helped him reach any conclusions, let alone offer relief.

Two things came out of this story for me. The first was it was the first time I heard someone telling my story, in this regard. The second was a deep conviction that I ought to write a book about how my thinking had changed, and how dark things had gotten, after two sharp blows to the head. I had been old acquaintances with everything we spoke of on the phone that day, some internal foe that over the years made me question my sanity altogether.

The sky burns a bright flame red, and I sit in a glass house, now, heating up. The sound of glass cracking, turning into fresh spider webs fills my ears. The house — this brittle and featureless cracking structure — is at the bottom of a strip mine, those desert kind that sit in the middle of a giant, looping spiral of roadway cut into the sides of the Earth, where I sit in this glass house. I can see a station wagon circling this roadway, headed down, down, with a huge dust cloud pouring off the back. A wheel is missing, and it's on fire. A skull face picked clean of flesh is behind the wheel, grinning, roaring wagon-wide circles, cutting its swath down the spiral, a parrot perched on its shoulder. The closer this ghost car gets, the more the cracks in the glass house grow… before I shoot up in bed. I am home.

****

I think, looking back, I had taken on my father's dreams. There were a few things my mother had shared with us despite normally being reserved and quiet. And so, when a story here or there about the earlier years of the family presented itself, it became something like folklore. The most pronounced of such stories was that my father had been working on some sort of table saw in the garage, back in the early 70s when we lived in Torrance, California. Maybe he had not been paying attention, maybe he had a couple of drinks before going out there to work on god-knows-what; what I do know to be true is that day he lost all his fingers at the last knuckle in a spray of bright blood. My mother wrapped his hand in some kitchen towels before trying to ease his shock and drive him to the nearest emergency room. Where the folklore begins — as they would tell it — is the larger of the two house cats, Big Kitty, ate the remains of his fingers scattered about the garage.

But the other story — far more pertinent to this chapter — was I was told years ago that when my mother was pregnant with one of us, my dad had been having a recurring nightmare. In it, he imagined himself fending off a giant fly that cornered him on a train. He kicked my mom square in the back, sending her flying onto the floor, before awakening and apologizing profusely.

In my own subconscious, I notice there are recurring themes in my cycles of sleep — somnambulistic entities appearing for bouts of time, often years, before disappearing — perhaps being resolved somehow in ways in which I am completely unaware. I have dreamt of drug abuse often, with the administration of said drugs always taking on peculiar forms. Sometimes, I am holding a burnt spoon with tiny, aquatic creatures swimming in it; sometimes, I am staring at a large, glass bottle with a nasty and razor-sharp fishhook at the end, knowing there is relief inside, but that I would bleed to death trying to get it. There, too, was the recurring dream of having been on an amusement park ride, a cavernous type; but rather than being pushed through a tunnel of singing marionettes, it was always a crumbling structure of torn, plastic tarps, rusted and rotting chains laying around, old boards with rusty nails poking out from every angle. In these, I find I have a gag tied around my head; I want to scream, but simply cannot.

Sort of an afterthought in the commission of this writing, I have taken to, essentially, drawing a map of my hometown as laid out in my subconscious. I find dreams can, often, be hard to remember. What is vibrant and fresh upon awakening is dulled or lost by the time I brush my teeth. As a result, I took on this project.

Each morning when I wake up, I take this calligraphy pen and large sketchbook drawing a map of where I lived, but as it appeared in that peculiar dream-state. The illustration looked a bit like one of those animated maps of Disneyland but with the features being themes I regularly explored in my sleep. There was the rat's maze of an underground parking garage with endless possibilities of getting lost downtown, the large spire building with an elevator that went two hundred floors up to where you would have to jump a chasm and risk falling to get into the building. There was the schoolyard full of ballistic missiles that would pop out of the ground; or the bohemian tree house shops that were hidden somewhere on Drachman Street where friendly vendors sort pottery, art, beaded things. Sometimes, they might offer me a golden ticket to a water ride, populated with singing animals that were always happy to see me again. But that one was hard to find, even though I was always looking for it.

I was never sure — not entirely — where all that darkness came from, how it engulfed my life for a long time, often leaving me shaken for the first hours as daylight came. And a great deal of it remains unto this day... I remember having a recurring dream of stumbling through a water-filled tunnel of sorts that opened up into a room. Crumbling walls of Earth with caverns opening up intermittently surrounded by what looked to be kids hand paintings one would associate with ancient ruins. I am always crawling through them, and somehow not wanting to. Every hole I crawl into, I am clear on one resounding idea: I am going down a tunnel, straight to hell, and there is nothing I can do to stop it.

****

When I hit fourteen, so much of what — at the time — were good things, things like my friend Jeremy, I shrugged off. I got turned onto punk and new wave back then, and from that early age, I began to compartmentalize things in my life: my cool punk friends over here, my childhood friends over there, anyone else I knew tucked squarely in its own category. I was terrified of the inevitable fact that somehow those groups might meet up, and collectively figure out, I was never who I pretended to be.

My sister met some friends — Rocky Horror type — that were into drag, makeup and new wave; I tried that for a while, and found it did not suit me. I was drawn to it, yet something a little bit darker, and a little bit heavier. I do not remember the last conversation I had with Jeremy, but what it amounted to was this: I've discovered something new, for now, and you are being discarded because I must do my own thing. We would not speak for another thirty years.

By the age of fifteen, our house was a haven for the scattered handful of deviants in our neighborhood. Mom would, often, come home after about a ten-hour shift at the small, outpatient hospital where she had been working to find the house full of cigarette or pot smoke, the couches re-arranged to our inebriated liking, or some kid with a Mohawk crawling in — maybe out — of our bedroom window, which, then, doubled as a front door. Kris and I took on watching the most depressing movies possible in marathons that lasted weeks, sometimes months; it was almost a triathlon to see who could sink lower into the murky depths of turmoil, as aided by film, and there were a number that we watched. My sister — for her part — was strong and much brighter than I, but she was working through her own things — haunts from her past — that would all but kill her.

The first few times I smoked marijuana I do not remember, well, feeling much of anything at all. There was an older kid from Catholic grade school who had given me, in retrospect, what might have actually been oregano. Who knows? Though it had little effect, it failed to dull my curiosity of just what that experience might hold for me.

I was at my second high school in sixth months. In the middle of a good bit of chaos I created for myself, I rediscovered freeing my mind, having been relegated to a small, classroom for alternative high school students, i.e. kids that — for a myriad of reasons — were having a tough go of it, tucked onto a much bigger campus of a much bigger school.

This is where I was to meet Mark, an older, pretty kind and overly mellow guy, two grades above me, who would spend mornings standing on this bridge passing over four lanes of traffic, his pipe tucked away in his palm, smoke wafting out his nostrils in tendrils, being coy and getting ready for the five-hour, minor workload ahead.

Up to that point, high school had been a rough ride for me; my time spent at Santa Rita was punctuated by a couple of nasty, well, 'initiations' is what they called them back then — a freeform hazing that, in my case, usually involved being a victim to someone else's violent idea of a comical time. And in truth, I brought that attention on to myself; as was usually the case with my injurious nature, they were self-inflicted wounds.

Having found punk rock from my sister and her couple of older friends made me a fresh and bright target for those looking for one, with my handmade t-shirts for bands like Flipper, and a freshly shaved head with a little bit of crimson stubble at that point. I was wearing a pleather jacket that looked like a motorcycle jacket with a few pins on it like DOA. The body of students had taken to calling me Kojak, which was usually resounded in statements such as, "We're going to fuck you up, Kojak." I was, often, deeply afraid, at the very least, nervous.

For whatever reason, this hippy fellow, Mark, and I had taken a liking to each other, and we were to be good, close friends for a few years after our exit from high school. Mark liked things like Jimi Hendrix, The Stones, The Doors — antiquated music that had never held any interest for me whatsoever but that I would grow to love all the same.

Mark was with whom I would concoct a series of experiments involving LSD, which was kind to me for a while, until it, too, unleashed a darkness in me that proved to be inescapable. But, in the beginning, we would carefully layout in our notes our means and plans for the weekend. One such time involved jumping rope with Christmas lights until we were sweaty and laughing and delirious, our pupils as big as saucers as a spray of rainbow tinged lights spiraled through my bedroom. Other times, it was a trip up to Sky Island on the mountain overlooking Tucson in my '71 Thunderbird where, on one occasion, low cloud cover had given us a vantage point to look down on a blanket of clouds, feeling like Gods. But all that was to come just a little bit later.

That year, I was a skinny freshman kid with a shaved head, always under duress of insults or verbal threats with some mild sliver of pride keeping me committed to a lifestyle that, for the time, meant standing out, something — looking back — that I always wanted. The first time I met Mark on that bridge, he asked me if I wanted to smoke. As stated, I had smoked before — or certainly thought I had — and nothing ever happened from it. It can only really be described, if anything, as a 'non-experience.' So, this day was no different in the way that I accepted the offer given me: to smoke a bit of pot before school, indulging both him and I standing there on the balmy, spring morning as traffic dashed underneath that bridge, taking a few deep pulls in, standing on that bridge, trying not to cough.

I remember, next, sitting in class and propping a book up in front of me, attempting to appear occupied. I had the sensation of quickly moving *downward,* as if the whole room was sinking rapidly below the Earth's crust. My chest felt tight, and I imagined the deep, rich symphony of bells clanging somewhere down below. I remember thinking that day, for the first time but most certainly not the last, "I am going to hell."

The year that followed, I explored the reaches of my own imagination day after day, smoking at nearly every possible chance afforded me, which felt a little bit like madness and impending mental collapse. That elevator sensation was always with me, and I would sit on the couch and close my eyes as visions of being chopped to bits and thrown into shark-infested waters clouded my mind, or being crushed flat by a hail storm of anvils dropping from the sky. I remember one day Todd, Jeff and I were at my mom's house, and we had smoked there all afternoon. I sat in a rocking chair, rocking slowly back and forth, my arms clutched to my chest, my head full of visions and thoughts of wild destruction and excruciating pain. Todd told me, "Dude. Knock it off man; you're creeping me out," but I was lost somewhere in my own interior, far beyond the typical giggling bouts and eating junk food, juvenile signposts that — for many — were simply a roadmap to adulthood.

Something peculiar that developed when I was young, around fifteen, around the time all the other trouble started, was almost an empathic and unwanted capacity to feel the **physical** pain of others. I was decades and lightyears away from becoming in-tune with how others felt, and how the weight and impact of my actions in and around their lives caused so many so much pain. Like I said, that would not arrive until **much** later.

But what *was happening* was watching something as simple as a medical procedure on the Discovery channel; it was like I could feel the scalpel ripping my own flesh, or feel a badly broken bone being reset. The feeling was always strong, and always left me with wild goose flesh and wanting to vomit into a bucket. And yet, somehow, at the same time, I was mildly fascinated by it. Whatever that was, was something that has stayed around very much to this day. In short, I have always had a very *physical reaction* and repulsion to violence, save for the sport of hockey which I very much enjoy.

By the time I was sixteen, a black cloud of tough luck hung around me. The light seemed too bright on occasion; 1 had a head filled with violence, and I was cast into the role of a young person unsure of where to fit but drawn inexplicably to darkness and to anger. My sister, for a time, was drawn to this crowd of cross-dressing, and new wave types with which I would tag along, and try to find some identity; and while all those people were nice enough, that did not seem like a good fit. Like a chameleon, I drifted to anything that reeked of subculture and mayhem, before finally, after having disguised myself as being both tougher than I was and more street-wise than I was, became the real thing. I suppose it was only a matter of time.

As all this went on, I watched my mother's life slowly erode under the weight of pressure, of what — at the time — appeared to be both her children in heavy distress. She went from playing tennis and golf on weekends, selling Mary Kay cosmetics and having make-up trials at the house and being an aspiring yet amateur photographer to rapidly becoming none of those things, to becoming a woman shaken to the core who found solace only in reading books, taking anti-depressants and going to bed as early as 7:30PM.

The house was beginning to bear the pockmarks in the measure of the mental health of those who lived there: the occasional broken window with a piece of wood in the frame until it could be repaired; fist sized holes in the drywall; a patch of burnt carpet where a candle had been left to burn on the floor all night. Kris was starting to write suicide poems in her room on the wall in black magic marker, and I had taken on a reckless and clouded lifestyle.

I had begun taking the city bus downtown at night and seeing these scrawls of graffiti in spray paint on walls and recycling containers all over town. In dripping blue paint, they said things like 'Opinion Zero' and 'Civil Order,' and I looked at them very much the way a detective might survey a crime scene: clues to something bigger, and an oasis for a young guy in desperate means of escape.

I would frequent a small record store on Sixth Street back then, and one day that I — a skinny fourteen-year-old kid — went in there, the record store owner, Joey Wrex, passed a flier across the front of the counter. On it, it said, 'PCP & Opinion Zero,' and in scrawl across the bottom, 'Two kegs of beer. Three bucks.' Joey told me, "Hey, this is later tonight. I think you should probably go."

My friend Dan and I walked around the university that night, and ultimately, sat at Greasy Tony's until six o' clock rolled around, before walking over to the address listed, which I remember as being 818 Speedway Blvd. Funny the innate details the mind holds onto, like precious gems.

We walked up Speedway and walked into a tightly packed back yard full of hooligans and the smell of warm beer: combat boots, leather jackets and spiked, belted denizens, many who I would find out lived here or crashed here, huddled in circles and brushed past each other. Everyone looked angry and threatening, and far older than I. Someone — who I would much later get to know as Dirty Burt and his band PCP — cranked up this wildly droning and heavy ended facsimile to music that made my teeth vibrate. It was my first experience seeing live music.

One guy dressed from 'Clockwork Orange' walked by with a snicker; another guy with double fin Mohawks filled my plastic beer cup and gave me a wink. "I don't know you," he said, and I did not know how to respond to that, so I went into the cramped and excruciatingly loud room with noise, and it was only later, we bribed someone with a twenty for a ride back to the east side. I knew then I brushed up against something that both excited and terrified me — this music scene that was so much bigger than my tiny life, and like a magnet, I was drawn to it.

For the next fifteen years, I would never think to look back.

****

I suppose I was up against the geographic misfortune that having come from the eastside of town loaned itself not at all to any type of street credibility. I was not raised near train tracks to be on the wrong side of, but rather, a golf course where refined and tanned businessmen, fitted in pressed khaki shorts and pink tops, spent their days improving their stroke. So, if only in this sense, my penchant for misfortune and being maimed or nearly killed in a couple of incidents served me well, in some ways loaning a larger-than-life Frankenstein-like appeal to my otherwise lacking 'street resume.' That and, for a time, I had a couple of cool cars that people I knew liked to ride around.

By nineteen or so, some of the pain of the rites of passage into adulthood were fading: the days of digging through my mom's medicine cabinet, to take thirty amoxicillin to try and feel anything at all, to ramming my fist through a door when I failed to get that relief. I did make the discovery of things that **did** — *in fact* — bring a sense of wellbeing, with the camouflage of who I thought I was and what I hoped to become, taking form.

I spent nearly all of my time downtown, and I spent a great deal of my senior year of alternative school sleeping in the back of my car in the school parking lot.

The high school I attended, Project MORE, was a small institution run by an older and tight-knit group of aging hippies who thought wildly outside-the-box in terms of education. They had a history credit entitled 'Famous Assassinations of the Twentieth Century,' or something to that effect, that appealed very much to my darkness, and a program for musicians called 'Rock School' fitted with all its own instruments, with a decent number of talented students in there every day abusing equipment.

The small punk rock population of that school was a group of death-wish kids who drove around in a Dodge sedan covered in

49

lime green spray paint that said 'corpse grinder' on it. They would often band together and crack open cans of Freon, roll up the windows and hallucinate in the school parking lot. It was probably a strong case of 'the pot calling the kettle black,' but whenever I was around them, there was a pervading sense that at any moment, someone was about to die; in this, my intuition proved to — eventually — be correct.

Tom, who had superglued a pot leaf to his forehead that year (which, later, turned into a nasty skin infection), and Larry, his best friend, both passed away in drug abusing episodes. Neither had been bright; both were dull-witted types, built for trouble. The ringleader, Mike, whom had owned the car and named the band they played in, was crushed to death by a piano some years later. At least, that was what I was told.

As such, I tended to spend my days in another huddle of students two years my senior on the other side of the parking lot. There was Greg Gooch who drove a wide collection of Morris Minors and antique Studebakers that his dad owned, Bill with his bright green Mustang, and Nikki who — if memory serves — moved to Arizona when her parents won the Chicago lottery. Nikka drove a Grand Prix and also, had a pretty heavy cast of darkness on her life, but we enjoyed the same types of music, and she was beautiful and always happy to hang out with me.

I was young, full of life and discovering new things; for a time, all was well.

****

Around the time I graduated high school, a few notable things happened in that particular period of time. I discovered amphetamines of all kinds, with the limitless inspiration they provided; I fell in love, maybe for the second time, since my grade school paramour, Kathy; and I had a terrible car accident.

The amphetamines, usually in the form of powdered brown crank — which back then smelled and tasted much like one would reasonable expect of cat piss — made me feel vibrant and alive. I would sit in an awkward crouch often for hours, fingering my guitar or bass, plucking through the same seven or eight notes with endless fascination for doing so, until my body was racked with cramps. I saw the world in bright colors, and meticulously went about painting everything that came across my path. The walls in my bedroom at my mother's were painted black, a small coffee table I fabricated orange, so on and so forth. Sleep and nutrition were left far behind to explore what I dreamed my own potential to be. Notebooks of to-do lists and drawn out projects lay scattered all over the floor, and I memorized catalogs of music, making mixed tapes with hidden messages — a cryptic 'hello' to those I thought could decipher them. I shed off pounds and nearly every bit of muscle mass from a childhood of abundance, and greeted a thousand sunrises wide awake.

In those dreamless and energetic cycles, I would often stay up for days working with plaster of Paris sculptures, life-like yet grotesque formations that I would, years later, abandon to an art gallery downtown owned by Steven Eye. He told me, much later, when I went to retrieve them that they had been eaten by rats and he had to throw them away.

My second love, Arah, I met at a house party. Arah had been — for the longest time — a Tucson girl but had recently joined a small migration of folks from our peer group who moved to the northwest; some went to be seasonal fisherman in Alaska; some went to be part of what a bit later would become an exploding music scene. I knew nothing of Seattle at the time and had never — in fact — even searched for it on a map.

There was this group then, led by the incredibly charismatic and fairly talented Odin, whose real name was Chuck. Chuck and his group of musicians — Dwayne, Spider, and a few others — had taken on the Celtic rock thing and had a group of young women who — when they played — would fan them with palm fronds and feed them grapes. I knew Arah to hang with that crowd long ago but had not seen or heard of her in years. As it was, this was the first time I think we ever spoke.

My first real work out of high school was helping this guy, Leonard Lyons, remodel and put together what was supposed to be a sports bar. Leonard was an alcoholic who was not drinking at the time, save for the O'Douls we always saw him with when he stopped by the strip mall where a handful of us were refinishing bar stools, sanding down this bar, and picking through the dust-covered remnants of the last tenant, to salvage what we could before the grand opening. Leonard, if memory serves, was going through a bitter divorce and had misconstrued some things on his business application to ensure his soon-to-be ex-wife would never see money from it. As it turned out, or so I would find out much later, he had lied to obtain his liquor and wine permit, and after all that work we put in that summer, he had to open a bar which served no alcohol. I heard it went under; I heard Leonard soon returned to drinking; I heard someone saw him pushing a shopping cart down the street a few years later, all his belongings in the cart, but that is just the word.

It was during this time, as the blazing summer was fading into the fall months and this job was winding down, that Arah and I met. She drove her Dodge Satellite with her dog and her four-year-old son down to Tucson to see her mom. For the two weeks she was there, we were inseparable.

We were around ten days in when she told me, "Hey. I have a question to ask you." Knowing our time was ending shortly, my heart already began to ache, pondering all that seemed like it was about to slip away. "Why don't you come to Seattle with me? Come up to live, if you want."

I did not take too much convincing, and I told my mother, who was dismayed, that I was moving to Seattle. We loaded up and brought along another friend, Mark, who decided he wanted to start fresh in Portland. We packed everything we could fit into the trunk, Mark and I, filled up the tank, and headed west on the Interstate 10.

****

We lived in Fremont, I think at 1st and 41st, right up the hill from an old rope swing on the channel, and about two miles from where I worked at a thrift store in Ballard.

Arah was working twelve-hour shifts doing nursing at a nearby hospital, and I, thus, found myself taking on babysitting duties for her, now, five-year-old son, for which I was insufficiently equipped; I knew nothing about kids, let alone how to take care of one. Truth be known, I was far too selfish and self-involved... and dark... to be hospitable to anything that looked like rearing up a young person in this world. I did not know it at the time, but I would make a significant amend to this young man two decades later, when he was having troubles of his own.

There were about ten of us from Arizona that would spend time together, and there always seemed to be someplace to go: the Tow Truck band in Queen Anne, Under the Rail, The Crocodile Café. Young people flocked to the city, some I remember meeting who hitchhiked from as far as Atlanta to try and be part of something much bigger than themselves; most ended up living on the street.

My drinking fell into full bloom in the absence of having done any speed for months; it was like an endless thirst was created, and microbrews invariably gave way to fortified wine. I always had a few before work, and as many as I could drink after. It did not take long before our little nest became an unhappy one; brimming with irresponsibility and fierce resentment. I began to struggle with sleep: two thousand miles from home with the vision of what we both hoped to be rapidly evaporating. It was here — I should make mention — that I first tried the needle.

Things came to a head the night before Halloween. I worked the closing shift at the Shop n' Save in Ballard, and there was about fifteen minutes left on the clock, as we closed at nine o' clock. A line of maybe ten paying customers stood at the counter, their arms having gathered the last accruements of whatever it was they hoped to round out their Halloween costumes. I was somewhere way in the back of the store, rummaging around, when two guys wearing black masks, Halloween masks, burst through the front door, waving guns in everyone's faces. My heart froze and instinctively, I went to the back, took my timecard, and clocked out, disappearing out the back door.

I went back, of course, and was not sure why I left. When I got there, a full police unit was on the scene, as was a firetruck. The manager — whose name I cannot honestly remember — had been struck across the face with a pistol at some point, and the police rallied around the remaining shoppers taking interviews.

I had two good friends who both worked at the store: Jeremy and Kirsten, who were engaged and soon to be married. We hovered around in the back room, and it was Kirsten who remarked, "Shit man. That was heavy, really weird." We had tentatively made plans to go to a party in west Seattle after work that night, and she brought that up: "do you still feel like going?"

I told her that after all that, I did not foresee myself getting to sleep anytime soon; so we agreed we would go to the party. I made mention that I did not have a costume, had not thought to get one, and she pulled a vinyl pre-packaged nun-outfit out of her shoulder bag. "Here, take this. I have an extra." I went to the small, cramped store bathroom with its naked bulb and cracked yellow tiles, and put on the costume which had that wonderful plastic smell I have always associated with new books and childhood.

We arrived at this party, just half a block from the beach, and were greeted by a packed house full of Kirsten and Jeremy's friends, a young and very professional looking crowd who fit the profile of those who would work at a law firm, would be quick to marry, and would jog through the park pushing a three-legged stroller. At least, that is how I imagined them.

There was a half keg of beer on ice in a tub in the kitchen, and a fleet of bottles on the dining room table of every sort: Tanqueray, Bacardi, a couple of different tequilas, expensive gin.

Liquor had been largely absent in my life as of that time, and yet it was what I loved most, more than anything. I loved the fast-acting warm rush; where swimming in confidence and bravado, I would change in minutes flat. Beer had always seemed too slow, even though — in hindsight — on nights like this one, liquor would be far too quick. Twenty minutes and three plastic cups, and I would evaporate from the party altogether...

I am being shaken awake by a hand on my shoulder, and another tapping me lightly across the face. "Hey you, hey. Hey you. Wake up. It's time to go." I lift myself up, blurry and half conscious. I had fallen asleep in the laundry room of this stranger's house. In fact, I had passed out up against the water heater which had melted some of the black vinyl cape to my leg hair. I could already feel the warm and very much sunburn-like sting going down my right side. This stranger who lived in this house found me, this unwanted stowaway in the blackness of his laundry room, and now, was inviting me to leave.

I stumbled out onto the tollway; the absence of traffic gave me the thought it must be in the early hours, maybe four in the morning. My esophagus felt hot, raw and itchy from hurling the last of my stomach into the bushes; my leg which has plastic still stuck to it, began to throb. I was a melted nun staggering up the beltway trying to get home. At some point, a gold Cadillac pulled over, the sound of its wheels softly coming up the embankment. The window rolled down.

"Hey, do you need a ride?" Blurry and tired, I accepted, and told the driver I was headed to Fremont. We rode along in silence, the cool saltwater air blowing in the window, which was still rolled down about halfway. The air felt cold, and good on my face. I felt awful.

"So…" The driver started, pausing. "Do you like to party?"

I told him, "Yeah, of course. I love to party. It's why I'm walking home," missing all social cues of what was to happen next.

I felt his big, meaty palm come down on my thigh and squeeze. Instinctively, I threw a weak and not-so-well-aimed punch that glanced his shoulder while shouting, "Get the fuck away from me!" The jerk jerked to a stop having just crossed the bridge. He told me to "get **the fuck** out!" I poured out the side of the car and halfheartedly threw a rock that missed altogether. The purple hue of sun yawning to life changed the sky in the east, and I walked. I was a mile from home.

When I walked in, I was greeted with accusations and Arah upset: upset that I did not come home; upset that I did not call;

upset that at 5:00 in the morning, I was banging around the kitchen. I shrugged her off, too tired to recall or even state the whole story: the armed robbery, the liquor, the car ride. But she was pushing it, *all of it*. I laid down on the couch, muttering for her to "fuck off" under my breath.

That set her off. Arah kicked me squarely across the face, lying there on that old plush couch, and I jumped up, adrenaline pumping, and I hit her. She looked shocked, and I felt equally so. She went to the bedroom and slammed the door. I laid down… now awake, my heart breaking. I remembered all those sweet, innocent things I stated about how I would love her forever, how I would never hurt her. And for the first — and the only — time in my life, I struck her, struck a woman. I knew then this was all over. I was leaving; I was going home.

I stopped on my way home — well, not on the way — to see my sister and brother in Manhattan, which lessened the sting, at the least, served for a distraction. I spent a couple of days with my sister, Gina, then working at the Museum of Natural History, who was one of a handful of paleontologists who were meticulously rebuilding the skeletons of everything in the dinosaur hall which, as it turned out, had been gerrymandered together with antelope and cow bones decades earlier when the exhibit was put up. I spent time chatting with her drinking espressos on the cool, urban streets and split time with my brother. He and I got in a jackpot one tonight leaving the Continental when I got so drunk, I could barely breathe; and we had to take a train back to Queens where he lived. They were like a fountain of life — those two — in what would prove to be a downward slope when I left a handful of days later to head back to Arizona.

****

Completely broke with no resources and a lack of ambition around career, I ended up back at mom's in the same old, black bedroom I had been in years before, the carpet still taken up, the rusted spring hide-a-bed still where I left it; the mattresses had all been ruined years prior.

Amphetamines quickly became a daily staple, again; only this time, I used them intravenously. I trembled and could barely keep my composure the first time I walked into a pharmacy and asked for a diabetic syringe. The pharmacist obliged with the huge, gauge needle likely for giving steroids to a horse, and rang me up for a dollar twenty-five. The end result was I was a mumbling and incoherent fool with giant bruises on my arms.

My mom suggested that I might look for work, and bought me a small, plastic-faced alarm clock with a second hand that audibly ticked away. I would sit there and stare at the wall, the ticking of that clock driving me slowly insane; I slept rarely, but when I did, horrific nightmares of being stuck in quicksand that slurped up around my neck and swallowed me whole, overtook me. My old artwork sat untouched, and my old friends were a fixture for whom I would occasionally make a cameo appearance after taking the two buses downtown to do so. The violence in my head overwhelmed and overtook me. From having been cynical and lonely, I became encased in and obsessed with the world of shadow.

One day, I was downtown walking, visiting a friend named Arlo who was always good for getting a shot of speed. Arlo had become transfixed on the idea that freemasons were somehow ruining his life, and saw a parallel universe of numbers and symbols that when he pointed them out, did seem a little peculiar.

That particular weekend, we had both been without sleep for far too long, listening to records, rambling incoherently about nothing. His house cat was giving birth in a closet, and we hunkered down and took it all in, the small miracle called life, completely out of our minds. When the sun came up a bit more, we went to the corner store to buy sodas. He glanced at the bottom of his can before opening it, and then pointed to a nearby license plate. The serial number on the bottom of the can said something like, 'QD556LPTY,' while the license plate said something like, 'DQ655YT.'

"They're onto us, man. The masons. Nearby, I can feel it," Arlo stated, with glazed eyes, sounding terrified. I doubted that, but it was fun to play along with his psychosis, so we talked of it for hours.

Soon, the sun was up, and overbearing heat, like an oven, radiated up from the sidewalk. I was walking, by myself now, and wearing a long sleeved flannel shirt. I rolled my sleeves up and feeling extremely self-conscious in the middle of my mania, looked down at my arms. Sick yellows and purples from self-abuse stared back at me, and I became aware and overly sensitive that somebody might see. I felt thirsty, and miserable, and crazy... I so badly wanted to roll me sleeves up and cool off yet feeling unable to do so; I was — in an instant — ashamed and mortified by what I had become. I sat down on some grass and started to cry. "Help me, help me to stop." I said, to no one in particular.

And I did, for a while. Three years to be exact.

****

As it was, a misdemeanor from a year or two prior was now catching up with me; but in truth, it was not so much the misdemeanor as my grievous irresponsibility in the handling of it, or lack thereof. I was offered forty hours of community service and a one hundred dollar fine to be completed in a year's time, with a few regular check-ins. It was the only and sole accountability anybody had placed on me, looking back, maybe ever; and I struggled to adhere to the expectations. I remember the look on the judge's face when I went before him one year later, an appointment set that was supposed to have resolved and squashed the case. He looked down his horn-rimmed glasses, his long beak holding them up, from his vantage point of an oak desk.

"Mr. Gould," he stated, "In the year I have allotted you to — in good faith — to complete a sum of forty hours of service to your community and pay a one hundred dollar fine, I see you have failed to complete these tasks. It looks here like you have done only eight of your mandated hours..." he paused. "And have made one payment, of five dollars."

He had me there. I shrugged my shoulders, unsure of what to say next, or what might happen. He told me, "I am resubmitting

58

this docket back to the court. In the meantime, you are to report to pre-trial services for mandatory drug screening, until the case can be re-addressed." The clerk handed me a green slip, and I was free to go about my business.

****

Common sense never was or has been my thing. I always liked to think it was a sign of a true genius to have such a busy mind that the doldrums of life would roll right by, going unnoticed, while the mind worked out much greater concepts, like how I imagined Picasso or Einstein to be. In my case, I am not so sure.

****

I was a bit surprised to find, after reporting to pre-trial for those three months, that the expectation had been I **stay sober**. All that time, I had been cursing my luck, thinking I had slipped between the cracks of some sort of legal limbo where my last accountability was uncompleted, and the new demands placed upon me were still to come. Hence, having gone from speed to abusing pills and heroin, it never occurred to me to think of giving a clean urinalysis.

I was told by the next judge, who had far less patience for me, I was being placed on supervised and 'direct' probation for a term of three years with lots of rules and a great deal of accountability, not the least of which was a surveillance officer, Wendy, who would intermittently check on me throughout the week to make sure I was where I said I would be.

Within a short period of time, sentenced to three years of abstinence and rules and turning in paychecks, I sank to a new low. Remorseful, evenings were spent on curfewed days staring at the weather channel for hours, my finger tapping the TV remote of endless possibilities, all of which I had no interest. The thought of a drink — just one — itched at me like I never felt; but having been caught already twice doing it, the threat of a short prison term was hanging over my head now.

I tried gaming the system in various ways, having learned to be a most skillful liar when I needed; but these folks saw right through me. One night, deep in a depression, I sat staring at a bottle of drain cleaner and a large economy-sized bottle of aspirin. The drain cleaner sounded like a wicked and violent way to go, which I could easily picture, as my thought-life for the last ten years had gravitated around morbid subject matter like that. The aspirin seemed like a big question mark. I had heard somewhere that "too much of anything will kill you," and without too many second thoughts, I made the feeble but dangerous attempt at eating about two hundred and fifty aspirin, which produced a sensation of the room turning upside down and a high pitched ringing in my head; the end result was a brief hospital stay, choking down charcoal fluid with the warning of kidney dialysis hanging in the wings. I received something between confusion and sympathy from my probation officer, who decided not to arrest me, even though my blood tests showed I simply cannot stay sober.

In the middle of all that, floundering and failing to meet the commitments placed upon me, being swallowed whole by my mother's house which was kept ten degrees warmer than necessary (to keep the electric bill down) and which never had cable TV, I was dying on the inside. What felt like a death sentence of boredom tinged with terror, I was coming apart. This led — of course — to more sneaked drinks which led to the neurotic fear of getting caught.

As such, it should not have come as a surprise when I walked into the probation office one Monday afternoon and was greeted with a warm welcome. The surveillance officer assigned to my case asked me to come down the hall to Ray's office, in what seemed like unusually quick timing as sometimes the wait was upward of an hour. I was dimly aware, as I headed back to see Ray, that I was flanked by another tall, muscular African-American officer who closed the door behind me when I walked in, greeted by a total of five officers: "Put your hands behind your back," one said. "You are under arrest."

The unmarked car glided through traffic as I sat in the back in loose fitting handcuffs, bewildered. I was explained that I had used up my chances; I was explained that I would go before the judge in a month; I was explained that the judge might opt to send me to prison, though probation would formally be recommending substance abuse treatment; I was, also, explained that I *could* sit in jail for up to one year's time, awaiting residential treatment where I would, also, be for one year. In short, I probably would not see home again for maybe two years. And, on some level, I would be lying if I said that did not come as a relief. I could not stand the way things were — nor had been going — for another second. I liked the idea of someday being different. I did not know then that I still had a long way to go until freedom came.

I took a deep breath and hunkered down for a long wait.

****

Jail, at least at that time, was not intolerable. I was placed in a low security unit with about a hundred and twenty beds partitioned off into four separate dorm rooms. The bunk bed I was assigned had a guy named Chuckie who looked very much like a cabbage patch doll, who would be here for the next six months for boosting car stereos; down a couple of beds was Mike Shank — his real name — who was caught with an ounce of cocaine and a handgun. He was a terrific dancer, among other things, and was always up to busting a few moves on his trips to the bathroom, and a wildly funny guy. He would end up doing five years, if memory serves.

It did not take me long to make some friends, Shad Thompson not the least of them, a slender and cocky guy with a loudmouth but who, also, was a lot of fun in a card game. Across from us was a guy who probably had defied medical science in every sense of the word as he had been shot point blank in the back of the head, and still had the bullet nestled deep in the center of his brain. Brian, who the others affectionately dubbed 'Bullethead Brian,' who had been shot over something involving selling or buying crystal meth; the result of that was a grown man who carried himself much like a six- or seven-year-old kid, often coloring on paper with drawing pencils in the day room, and whom seemed perfectly adjusted to this dreary life in institutions.

****

I step onboard the Greyhound bus, tucked beneath the other large, steel chassis, its engine belching smoke, idling, waiting to whisk us away; I look over my shoulder, mildly paranoid, perhaps more than necessary. The probation department will not know for a day or two that I have absconded, that I have failed to stay sober, that I have abandoned my hopes of having a successful legal outcome.

I don't think it is so much my flight from law that has me paranoid — though this happened to be the big fact of the day — but rather, the intravenous cocaine I've been using. My ears ring like tornado sirens; my palms sweat; and I vacillate between chatting up near bystanders on any matter of subjects, to going ghostly quiet reading far too into my surroundings. I see that I have forty minutes until my bus departs, and I walk around that run-down part of downtown with something in my hand that I intend to send. I stopped on the way here, to purchase it, and stuck a stamp on it as well. It is a Thank You card, and this is what it says:

> *Dear Ray,*
>
>> *I know you were in my corner always. And I know you care about me, and you've done nothing but try to help. Please forgive me for taking off, and giving up on all you guys, but I need to go get myself figured out. Maybe I'll come back some day, but I wish you the best. And thanks again for everything.*
>>
>>> *Signed,*
>>> *Jeff*

I find the remnants of a broken, ball-point pen on the ground, and scrawl across the envelope the address of Adult Probation with a 'care of' wedged beside it. At this point, everything about me needed work, including my handwriting. I did not know it then, but this would not be the last time I would see that card. *I stuff it into the large, blue, metal drop*

box and shuffle my way back up the street to the bus terminal. The bus, as it
turns out, is now boarding. I present my ticket, and step on board.

My plans are flimsy and riddled with fear. I will go back to Long Beach,
maybe Torrance, or maybe Venice. I will search for something — anything
— that feels like home. I knew — or rather did not know — that
whatever I was searching for was not going to come. Los Angeles
was not my home; in fact, it was a vague recollection at best: a
dusty, old impression that had faded out altogether. I was going —
as I was told later — to be swallowed whole.

NO BEAST SO FIERCE PT II

My body intermittently tingled with cold sweat, hot flashes, dope-sick pangs which had me double over. My biology was a living laboratory: add some of this, or some more of that, skating through fields of unwanted effects. I was growing more and more ill as the bus pushed forward through tiny and crumbling landscapes marked only by tall weeds, truck stop super centers, and the occasional train cutting across the landscape.

I stopped in Phoenix to see my friend, Rick. I had been using heroin again for only two weeks, and my body was overwhelmed with sickness. Rick's son, Miles, six at the time, engaged me in his interests. He showed me drawings, things he liked to play with, a skateboard trick he was trying to learn. He referred to me, perhaps for the first time, as "Uncle Jeff."

"Uncle Jeff," I remember him saying. "Are you sick? You look sick. I feel bad for you, Uncle Jeff."

Such a bright kid, Miles was. He knew I was in bad shape, and I felt that tug at my heart a little bit. He was, I remembered, the first infant I ever held in my life, and in some respects, the first time I marveled at life itself in doing so. Prior to that, babies seemed like gross, squirmy little things that took up energy and attention. It was not until six years before, as I held onto Miles in Rick's backyard that I saw the tiny person inside, looking up in awe and amazement, coming awake to a life that had just begun.

Rick and I spent a couple of days going to bars, though the drugs had taken over by that point, and the drunken blur of good times past sounded like the last thing I wanted. I was morose; I was scared; and I was, now, officially homeless. The brittle dream of beginning a new life by the sea was starting to be shot through with the holes of reality, neon signposts that told me wherever I was headed, a small, cozy house by the ocean was probably an illusion.

We went to see Rick's roommate's band one night, The Beelzebullies, who punched out a high paced vibrant set, then returned to Rick's townhouse where we smoked and created elaborate sarcasm well into the morning. I slept in Miles' room, who slept with his dad. Hour after hour, I laid beneath the covers, huddled in with a flashlight, injecting shot after shot into my arms, until sleep came.

On day three, I opened up to my friend Rick, who knew — knew all too well — something had gone horribly wrong with his old friend, but he had probably not known to what extent. I was rarely that forthcoming with the facts of my life.

"Hey brother," I said, my eyes filling up with tears. "I'm gonna be sick, and it is going to be bad, and I got to stop this shit before I go to Los Angeles."

It was that morning, too, that I had called my mother — now worried sick — to tell her I left the halfway house. She was in tears almost immediately, but not surprised. I had become a series of bad news, each day for the past ten years, my own personal headline, in chaos and heartbreak both. This was merely more of the same, and my assurances that I would get a house soon and send pictures of the beach, seemed to fall flat over the phone. We talked just another minute or two and hung up. We would not speak again for some time.

66

The next morning, I looked through the phone book, looking for resources to try to get myself together. The LARC program, a county detox, had an address listed on Van Buren Street. I stuffed my few articles of clothes into my backpack, and we jumped in Rick's truck to drive downtown where he would drop me off, and I would have to figure out the remainder of the way. Van Buren was a shoddy and infested place: broken boarded-up windows bearing tagged graffiti of the multiple gangs who patrolled; dirt blankets and empty wine bottles at bus stops; unhappy couples screaming at each other from behind closed doors of battered, little units with broken children's toys scattered across the front yards. I pushed my way up the street, ignoring any manner of passerby, starting to sweat and to come unglued in the insufferable heat.

I walked a mile, maybe two, before I saw what looked to be a giant limestone structure with great spires and towers, looking wholly out-of-place in the sense of architecture, yet blending right in with the surroundings if only in the sense that I had come to the right place, and with the feeling that good things probably did not happen here. What caught my eye, as I fumbled around for the address I had written on a slip of paper, was a banner across some tall, steel fences near what looked like a manned and gated post. This, is what it said:

'REHABILITATION STARTS HERE'

I realized I arrived, or thought I had, and with my backpack slung over my right shoulder, I walked up to the guard post. "Hi…..um, I'm here." I stated, making reference to the fact that I called ahead.

"You are where? Here?" the uniformed guy manning the post said, devoid of all expression behind his mirrored sunglasses.

I asked, "This is the LARC, correct?"

He told me, no it wasn't. It was the State Hospital and the Alhambra processing prison but informed me the detox unit was one building down. As I made my way to the other gate, a DOC bus with thin slits for windows brought in a fresh group of inmates, turning them over to whatever faced them inside.

The detox unit shared some areas with the state hospital where those who had been acquitted of serious crimes on a basis of insanity were, also, kept. I remember hearing the faint and distant echoes of someone screaming bloody murder as I was led up the yellow, antiseptic hallway through a series of locking steel doors. Though I was there voluntarily, it felt anything but.

We were housed in a series of partitioned off cubicles in a large concrete room that looked very much like a spoked wheel. In the center was an observation station with what might have been shatterproof glass, encasing observers in, and we laid there on cots covered with old, thin, white sheets; I was explained upon admission, we were there for a "twenty-four-hour observation period" to see if, in fact, we became symptomatic and needed to be medicated. A couple of beds down from me, an older guy chattered on about re-runs of old TV shows... talking to no one, or anyone, while a few beds from him another alcoholic, in the grips of delirium tremors, began screaming at him to shut up. I laid there quietly, curled up in a ball, trying to think of places other than there.

A handful of hours after being assigned my bunk in this windowless and otherwise featureless room, a tan-skinned and very tattooed street tough was placed in a bunk next to me. I laid there — in my own world — while a nurse with a cart came around and passed out bologna sandwiches.

Another few hours passed, and I was jarred awake by the tattooed guy, the Latino kicking the leg of my bunk. He asked me if I took his bologna sandwich, and my guts felt queasy, sensing trouble coming as he spoke. I told him I did not. He asked me, again, and pointed out, "Well, it didn't just fucking walk off, and it's just you here." Before I could respond, the nurse who pushed the cart hours earlier stepped in: "No, it was me who took it back. I thought you didn't want it." *Sigh of relief.* He apologized and told me his name, and I told him mine.

I was not sure how long exactly had passed, but the twenty-four-hour period had crawled by, and frankly, I had enough. "Listen man," I told him. "Can you get dope?" I told him that I sewed some money into my wholly jeans covered in patches of various types. "I got forty bucks. Let's get the fuck out of here, and go get something."

He agreed. We left.

I laid down in the back seat of his Corolla, and Spanish Norteño music poured out of the small and crackling car stereo speakers. He told me to "get down and stay down. We're going to see the Sandman, and where we're going, white people... they just can't go."

I did as I was told, and twenty minutes later, we sat in an empty and dusty lot, limbs growing warm and heavy, swimming with dragons chasing our thoughts. "Can you drop me at the Greyhound bus station, brother? I have a bus to catch." Two hours later, I was on the Interstate 10 headed west, my head still floating and pressed up against the glass.

****

The bus winded through the inner city of Los Angeles, and I chose to wait a couple of stations before decided to step off somewhere around Hollywood & Vine. I marveled at the soft, saltwater air and the yellowish glow that floated like a blanket hovering the city; the lights of far off cars disappeared as they twisted up winding roads into the Hollywood Hills. It smelled like Durham cigarettes, and felt like a carnival.

I walked a bit up the Avenue of the Stars, some cracked and under construction; some passersby were littered on the sidewalk playing bongo drums, or sitting with their heads lowered in wheelchairs. The well-dressed and cosmopolitan passed by in groups of seven or eight, their laughter filling the night. Pretty soon, the professional familiar pack of dressed up superheroes started to appear as the lights and majesty of the Chinese Theater drew me.

I had unearthed the rest of the cash I had, out of various hidden compartments in my backpack and sewed into my clothes. I had exactly one hundred eight dollars left, the remnants of my last paycheck from Artisans where I had worked as a prep-cook.

I looked at it, frowning. I knew if things got bad enough, I might sell my grandfather's WestPoint watch, probably the only thing I had on me of real value, besides my blue, leather motorcycle jacket.

I was twenty-seven, but look a bit younger, and gangly; so it was good that my license was intact. I headed over to Sunset Strip not knowing, really, where I was going, or what I was to do. So, I went to the bar.

After a handful of drinks, I chatted up a local guy, who turned out to live in the San Fernando Valley, a good miles away. I told him my half-baked plan about getting an apartment, not going home to face down the legal snare that I got myself into, really, about making a fresh start on my hundred and eight bucks. He must have felt sorry for me because he offered me a place "for one night only," and despite my suspicions that he might have some awkward, ulterior motive for bringing me there, I took his offer. I think he was just drunk and wanted to talk. I do remember in the morning though, he looked at me and stated flatly, "Good luck. This city is going to eat you alive..."

The next couple of days were park benches and a trip to Santa Monica where I fancied drinking myself to death, or throwing myself into the ocean until saltwater filled my lungs and the riptide took me away for good; but neither was to happen that day. I drank a $3.99 pint of crap vodka, and took a bus back into town, aimless, with a fresh sense of dread and loneliness washing over me.

In typical fashion of how I lived back then, I located the number of a teenage girlfriend who moved to L.A. to be a drummer, and who did play in a few bands. Naïvely, I simply expected that my tale of woe would be matched by an offer of a place to stay for a few months; but it turned out, Suzie already had seven or eight roommates and was getting ready to go on tour in Europe with her newest band. This felt like a crushing defeat.

It was like that a couple more days, not really sleeping, dozing off with my head against my knees, usually tucked behind a wall somewhere, but always hyper alert and startled at even the slightest noise nearby.

In my first week or two, I met a few Swedes living in L.A. attending a music production school. They were a hard drinking bunch whose apartment was littered with beers cans, beer bottles and pizza boxes, who told me stories of pretty much living endlessly off of student loans, by way of the Swedes approach to educating its citizens. I do not remember exactly what they said, but it was to the effect that they could choose any major they liked, and the government would pay for housing, school and cost of living, provided they paid ten percent of whatever they earned for life and provided they got a job in the same field as their degree. These guys knew a good thing when they saw it and switched majors multiple times before going to a school right smack dab in the middle of Hollywood, owned by ESP Guitars. They had a healthy skepticism around letting me stay much longer than a day here or there, as they should have, but we would get well-oiled a few nights a week and stay up all night talking about music. They played in two separate bands, a cover-song Motorhead tribute called Moosehead, and another politically-driven outfit called Time Out.

On a day when I was not keeping company with them, I watched the sun go down hanging out in a park with nowhere to go, somewhere off of Sunset Strip. I took off my leather jacket and slung it over a fountain while sitting there staring at my hands when I saw the silhouettes of five or six guys crossing the park heading my way. They had a certain swagger, a confidence, that I associated —correctly so — of predators looking for prey. As they got closer, it became pretty clear quickly: these guys were gangsters, and they found their mark.

"Yo-Yo, what's up? What's up, homeboy?" the obvious chieftain said, eyeing the others carefully as they spread around, flanking an exit I might hope to make. The turning in my gut and the tension in my shoulders prepared me for the blows that were coming soon. He asked me again: "I said, what's up? What are you doing in our park?"

I fumbled for words, barely making eye contact, a wave of self-pity striking me as my mind raced for something, anything to say.

For some reason, the only thing I could think to say was,

"Nothing's up, man. I'm homeless, and hungry, I'm not from here, and sorry if I'm in your spot when I'm not supposed to be." I took a deep breath and winced, expecting a hook to come at any moment.

"No shit man," the leader of this group said, "I feel that." He fished around in his sagging, oversized pants for a moment and pulled out a subway token: "Listen man, listen here. You gotta take you the red line train, go downtown. Get off, and walk three blocks up the way, and take a left. There's a spot there — Transition House, they help folks like you, man." And he put a subway token down on the fountain beside me. "You ought to take care man. These streets is some scary places," he said. And with a motion of a finger, they walked off, the six of them, and I sat there, looking at that token.

The next morning, I descended the stairs of the Hollywood train station through the street musicians and cross dressers, some eccentric older lady walking a poodle wearing a hand-knit sweater, to board the train. I double checked the faded map on the subway wall to make sure I did not get turned around, and got on the red line a few minutes later, headed downtown.

I arrived at my stop, and walked up from the subway tube to the smell of fried street food mixed with what seemed to be collard greens and soiled alleyways. Old, brick buildings from the turn of the century had signs stuck in the windows, some handmade for haircuts, or cashing checks without ID.

I remembered what I was told, and proceeded walking up this alley, a narrow-choked roadway with garbage bags piled up in mountains, odor filling my nostrils. This place shouted wildly of the failures of mankind and reeked of inattention. Somewhere, a man with no legs mumbled to himself in what sounded like Latin; a homeless woman who appeared to have grave mental illness sat among the trash heap, turning the pages of a pornographic magazine. I clutched my backpack a bit closer and marveled at where my path had brought me.

I went up and around the corner to the left, as I was instructed, and walked up the steps on Wilshire to the T-House. I was shown to a bunk, and surveyed the room which held about fifty or sixty bunk beds, not unlike a jail. Each man was given a drawer or two, and a small cot with a grey disaster blanket on it. I noticed only one other Anglo resident, and forty-five or so black guys, playing cards, laying down, or getting dressed to go look for work. I had not been there long, and someone came and gave me an elbow, "You been tested yet?"

I blinked: "What? I don't know... what you mean."

He said, "You know, tested, TB test. Place up around da co'ner pay you ten dollaz to take a test. They give you twenny five if yo shit comes back hot, man." He continued: "Lemme show you. Right up over dair, 'round da co'ner," pointing out the window.

By this point, I had no money left; hell, I had nothing, and ten dollars seemed like a pretty good bet to have an oversized needle shoot a bubble of air up under my skin. I remembered the process; I had one as a kid, and it made me puke.

When I returned, a rough looking — and smelling — group of guys lingered around counting their money, also having just come from the TB clinic. One guy, a lean and tall older black gentleman, could not believe his "good fortune" when he came back with not ten in hand but the full *twenty-five*.

"Thank you, Jesus," he said. "Thank you for the extra fifteen dollars." A few of the others looked down at the couple of five-dollar bills in their own hands, clearly unhappy with their own take. One handed a small, brown, paper bag to the older guy, the infected one.

"Hey man, breathe into this bag. I gotta get me some of that. I need that extra fifteen dollars, man, c'mon." That's just how it was in a neighborhood like that.

The Transition House was not to be the bedrock upon which I would form a new life. Feeling wildly like the odd-man-out, having been the sole apologetically white person in the dorm, since the other guy had taken flight, I was beginning to feel like a target; and wherever I belonged in this world, somehow Skid Row did not seem like the place for me. I packed up the few things I had in my green backpack once more, put on my motorcycle jacket a bit too warm for Los Angeles, (but I felt it made me look tougher than I was) and I left.

I had not been in Hollywood long before I was approached on the street by a well-dressed gentleman in a sweater vest who looked shifty and out of place in both his mannerisms and attire. He explained to me he had just gotten out of treatment, having been in some sort of a drug program for the past year. He told me he was from Detroit and asked if I knew where to 'score.' I told him I did but that it was not nearby, and it would take us subway to get there. I knew it because I had just come from there. And, so, I was back on Skid Row for the second time in a week, this time around as a consumer.

We took the train downtown, and this guy was growing shiftier by the minute, perhaps that someone from his program would see him, or perhaps that someone would see him *with me*.

We climbed the stairs leading up to the street from the underground rail system and made our way to Skid Row. Small, vinyl tents and sleeping bags littered the sidewalks on all sides. Burnt and ashy trash barrels had faint pops from the fires of the night before, and the entire street smelled of human waste and garbage. Places like this — really, communities like this — have their own quiet set of politics governed by violence and intimidation for those who called this place home. Dope — heroin that is — goes for seven dollars a bag there, usually fished out of someone's mouth where they have been "cheeking" it so they could swallow their payload in case the police came for a shake down. I always found that weird, seven dollars, that it was not a more even number like ten.

We bought two clean syringes and a handful of bags of dope, and left as expediently as we could; just the act of pulling out money on this street was akin to moths circling a luminescent light, and it was best to go, and quick. The dope looked odd to me, like something you might fish out of a cat box: a black and white speckled blob, slow to dissolve, that was cut with something that made your face go numb.

We trained back to Sunset, and no sooner had we gotten high in a small, cheap hotel room than this well-dressed gentleman — sweater vest and all — had a personality change so drastic — *in seconds flat* — that made it apparent, I should leave, now, which I did.

I glided down the street, in elusive consciousness, before a heavy weight settled in over taking my limbs and drawing me down to the concrete in the relative safety of a doorway. My stomach jolted, and the contents of my lunch emptied itself from my belly.

Outstretched, warm and motionless, I laid there for some time before something going past got my attention. As I laid there on my side staring out at ground level, I noticed a clean pair of black, leather boots tucked into black cargo pants; it was a rugged, urban look, and its walk seemed to have purpose. Turning my head up a bit more, I saw a belt harnessed with a flashlight, what appeared to be a handheld radio, and what looked like forceps with rubber gloves tucked into his back pocket. The black t-shirt covering this muscular frame said, 'Los Angeles EMS.' I knew, maybe just for a moment, what I wanted to be. Then, I faded out altogether...

I might have considered it good fortune: it became clear after five weeks or so, I would not get an apartment any time soon; I would not be rebuilding a new life by the ocean; and whatever this place was, it certainly did not — as I had once hoped — feel anything like a homecoming. My stubborn hubris and naïve insistence on how things would be was no match for my actual circumstances; things gradually got worse every day.

It was somewhere in those last couple of weeks, ore and defeated, I would step into a pawn shop off Sepulveda and surrender my grandfather's WestPoint watch for forty dollars. At the time, it was the sole item passed along to me as an heirloom, and it stung my heart greatly to let it go. I would phone mom collect every few days, and these were sullen and short conversations. I tried to tell her about my new Swedish friends, and how I thought things might really be looking up for me, but I think we both knew otherwise.

After a handful of weeks, she told me my sister, Kris, would be travelling to San Diego to receive some type of award for her merits in education. Kris, mom, and one of Kris' best friends would be making the five-hundred-mile drive out. I fumbled around for words before finally asking: "Do you think you could pick me up? Would that be alright?" I heard a long pause on the phone before my mother told me: "Sure." I wanted, more than anything, to go home.

****

The car ride was long and quiet; the windmill farm outside of Palm Springs, which usually inspired some type of conversation, even that fell flat. I sat, hanging my head in shame as my sister quietly burned in resentment: yet another of her life events hijacked by rerouting to rescue me from my poor life choices. This, obviously, was not the first time, and it would take years to mend this wound.

Back home, I hung around the Double Zero bar in the evenings, trying to find the right tincture of liquor, pills and white powders to screw up the nerve to turn myself over to the authorities, having an active warrant for my arrest, and no good options in front of me; but the mixture to gather the resolve to do it seemed elusive to me. Sometimes, I ended up sitting all night on a sidewalk and sleeping behind a building; while other times, vodka mixed with cocaine inspired a fresh burst of courage and inspiration to buck the system altogether, with some flimsy idea of getting a fake birth certificate and new identity. Looking back, I am certain that the new identity would have had just as many problems as the old one, perhaps more so. I informed the circle of friends that still kept my company but after three weeks of leeching off their bar tabs, and sometimes sleeping on their couches, they began to express their doubts that I had any intention of facing up to having broken my probation.

I think about three weeks had passed, my welcome being worn out, and the certainty that if I was picked up for anything

— anything at all, say, jaywalking — the outcome would be much, much different than if I went to rectify things myself. I contemplated all this, from the safety of a bar stool at the Double Zero and looked in my wallet. I had four one-dollar bills… just enough for two long island iced teas and no tip.

I ordered the drinks and knocked them back. That warm, soft glow of cheap, low-shelf spirits hit me, and if only for a minute, gave me courage and clarity. I asked if I could use the bar phone, and the bartender, looking askance at my four dollars sans tip on the bar, said sure. I called 9-1-1. "Oh, hello there. Listen… I'm a *fugitive,* and I wish to surrender myself over to the authorities this evening." I liked that word, fugitive; it inspired visions of some rogue agent operating out of boundaries, perhaps with a gun in his sock. The word must have been well-placed because it clearly got the attention of the operator at the other end of the line.

"Where are you now, sir? We will come pick you up."

I said, "No, how about this? Meet me at the Ronstadt bus terminal in twenty minutes. I'll be there, with a green backpack." She started to reply, and I hung up. It was 10:30PM, and I started my walk, just a half a block really, to whatever awaited me when I got there.

Downtown Tucson was dark and quiet, a somewhat bustling banking and commuting — mixed with several other things — by day and save for a few open bars at night; that, and most of the buses had quit running already so it, too, was equally deserted.

I walked all the way into the center of the terminal, near the ticketing counter, when I was suddenly awash in floodlights coming from every direction. A half a moment later, a helicopter appeared over the tops of the low apartment buildings, blinding me in a feverish white light. For a second, I thought maybe fugitive had been overkill. From a loudspeaker mounted on a patrol car bellowed, "SIR, PLACE YOUR BACKPACK ON THE GROUND.. GET ON THE GROUND. SPREAD YOUR AMS AND LEGS WIDE, AND WAIT FOR FURTHER INSTRUCTIONS."

I did exactly as I was told, placing my backpack on the ground at my right side, with an old Sony Walkman and a few cassettes and maybe some t-shirts and a toothbrush in it, and pressed my face against to the cool and grainy complexion of the concrete. And just like that, I was back in jail, again.

Something I learned, at least that time around, that the jail intake process, which usually takes twenty-eight hours of holding in tight, cramped quarters with ten or eleven guys for one stainless steel bench and only bologna sandwiches is quite deliberate. I had been through that process a half a dozen times, and it never seemed to get any easier, nor any more comfortable. What usually might have been more than a twenty-four-hour stretch of standing with my back against a wall took maybe less than ninety minutes. I will never know, but I wonder if someone in charge who was familiar with my call thought, "This guys is trying to do the right thing. Let's cut him a break on the hellish hazing of the intake process." The few inmates I did talk to in that ninety-minute period were somewhere between disbelief and disgust that a guy would turn himself in. One said, "I can't believe it. You snitched yourself out."

I kept quiet, to myself mostly, reading a few Reader's Digest magazines and reading Watership Down for the fifth time, a staple of any jailhouse library, waiting for the time to pass as my court date was still three weeks away. When the date did come, I heard through my public defender that the probation office stated they were grateful I had done the right thing. And so, alongside another twelve men who were shackled next to me, I went to find out my fate.

I was maybe sixth or seventh in cue, waiting for the guy ahead of me to explain that his domestic violence charges were merely a significant misunderstanding, when it was finally my turn to approach the bench. I felt a huge lump in my throat, and it seemed like my feet turned to glue.

"State of Arizona versus Jeffrey Gould. Approach the bench, Mr. Gould." I stood up, and still chained to the other unfortunate souls, stood behind the oak podium where I faced whatever came next.

"Mr. Gould," the judge said, staring me down. "Mr. Gould, I want you to know something. I've seen a lot of people run in my time, presiding in this court, many times. But I have never..." He paused staring at me. "Never, not once, have I seen one of those men send a Thank You card." And suddenly, as if on cue, he lifted that card I dropped in the bus station addressed to Ray some seven weeks before, which had been safely tucked between his case notes.

"And, as such," he continued, "I think I would like you to have another chance at Intense Probation for a one-year term." I winced; I wanted this to be over, really, years ago but accepted what he said. I was to be remanded to a house on Hedrick Street, the same place where I resided when I left. Back to the same thing, starting over, once again.

****

That fall, back at the halfway house, at least for a bit, the spirit of life was breathed back into me; and I had found and taken up a new interest, and that interest was going to the community college on the far southeast side to attend an EMT course that was available. My life for the next nine months became a simple one. I woke up at 5:30AM, headed over to the main part of the property where, every morning, a hot breakfast was served, and usually ate with one of the other eighty-eight guys who — like myself — had some degree of legal consequence hanging over their head and were either looking for a way out or biding their time until it was up.

At about 6:45AM, I walked over to the bus stop right in front of the Jack-in-the-Box where, recently, one of the residents - a guy I knew well — had died. The story there was he had been stripped down to his boxer shorts one night, psychotic, and trying to smash the windows of the restaurant out with a shovel; when the police showed up to restrain him and took him down, his heart exploded from whatever it was he had been on. I always thought of that incident, standing at that bus stop on those early mornings, waiting for my seventy-five-minute bus ride to where I would partake in class all day.

There were a pair of sisters, Hannah and Natalie, that took my class, also, and we all but immediately paired off into a study group with a well-rounded index of inside jokes that the class seemed to loan itself to, many of which revolved around anti-pneumatic shock trousers like, "I would love to get into her anti-pneumatic shock trousers," I would quip as some random girl in the cafeteria walked by.

Hannah drove a blue Camaro and had a daughter who was functionally deaf, whose father was a guy I knew years before who hung around the same late-night rock and roll scene with the same crowd I used to run. Months later, that the younger sister, Natalie, told me, "People like you break my heart, and I don't want anything to do with you ever again." But at that point, we were all still, seemingly, the best of friends.

I always found when I cared about something, I could easily give it my full attention, and the morbidity of the things I was studying, coupled with my deep fascination for hard science, made this easy subject matter for me. Like the others, I made flash cards and marked my heavy text book with page markers in bright pastels; perhaps unlike the others, I would find terms that rhymed with other terms, and try and fit material we were to be tested on into song lyrics. I would, then, memorize the lyrics. I may never remember what it was, but I had about a third of the test material laid out to the tune of ABBA's "Fernando."

The skills demonstrations of compressing an arterial bleed or transporting someone with compound fractures, things involving airway obstruction, I was about average. But when asked to, first, draw a human heart, and then, trace how a drop of blood moves through it, the artist in me rose to the occasion, and I performed a task like that with the greatest of ease.

In the back of my mind, I kept thinking, *I knew little about recovery from addiction, but I knew enough to know that somehow, it had something to do with helping people.* I convinced myself my interest in scraping bodies off the road, post car accident, would be enough. As it turned out, I, still, had much to learn.

Around that time, I was hired at the Sausage Deli, a small, family-owned sandwich place that maintained its location on Grant, right about on the line between the college kid neighborhood and where things right across the street took a turn for the worse, in what might best be described as "white trash gone wrong" for a few miles. I did not love the job, but I did have my own tiny prep room and demonstrated enough responsibility to be able to take on a couple of additional duties, like helping to place orders through the major food distributors by way of taking inventory. I worked three or four days a week, went to school for another three days, and was up until midnight most nights studying, sans any social life or, really, the need for one. My social life never had involved being sober, on any level.

One thing I might mention, which had at that point, been a struggle: directly across from the Hedrick House's sprawl of duplexes and units that housed several dozen sat a small, white house where one of my best friends and running partners, Doug, lived with his girlfriend, Casey. Doug, affectionately known as 'Dugga Dug,' was probably the best drummer I have ever met. He and I had great misadventures together and had both been in a punk band called Backstab Gospel just a few years prior. Every time I walked to or from the tiny unit that I shared with six other guys, the thought of sneaking across the street, maybe to "cut loose a little" was always there. We saw each other on the street every once in a while, and I tried not to linger, as my palms would get clammy and I would feel my heart start to race; I physically reacted to the idea of 'getting something going,' if nothing else, both in my flesh and my lizard brain tucked neatly away in my brain stem, remembering what relief felt like and craved it. But for now, I forced myself — over and over — to do the right thing daily.

As the year wore on, my EMS class was both encouraged to do an ambulance ride-along and also required to seek out clinical rotations, voluntarily shadowing nurses or hospital staff in any one of the five major hospitals scattered through our small city.

There was St. Mary's, known for having the best burn unit, while St. Joseph's was known best for pre-natal care; TMC was known for being a hospital that architects decided a one-story major hospital might be a neat idea — the only one of its kind in the country — but it, like UMC, was a Level 1 Trauma Center, complete with helicopter pad and all. And then, of course, there was Kino, which was known for doing heavy psychiatric care, the kind of place where people mumbled incoherently on street corners or lashed out at phantom government agencies, where people would end up usually by way of a court order.

Our classmates, almost universally, jockeyed for different rotations at Kino, wildly fascinated by the unhinged and unstable. For myself, these types of people had been the window dressing for a lifestyle I had long maintained, and I naturally gravitated to the trauma: something inside me — going way back to early teenage years and dark thinking — wanted to face down the past somehow and make peace with my own interior, for whatever that might mean. I made sure to call ahead and set up my first clinical rotation at St Mary's on the overnight shift.

I took the bus over to the west side and stopped to get a cup of convenience store coffee, a little too warm and with that bitter rust-taste from having sat on a heating element all day, but it would keep me up at least halfway through the night, so it was good. I mentally calibrated a number of things taking the bus over there, and categorically arranged them: things I hoped to see, like gunshots, for example; and things that might be better if I did not see yet, or maybe never see at all, like anything involving wounds to the genitalia which made my skin crawl just thinking about it. I looked down at my scrubs and felt **almost** *professional,* and almost like an actual person altogether.

I was greeted by a friendly CRN at the desk, who had in her notes that I would be coming, and told me I would get to spend the first few hours with her in triage doing basic assessments and determining both priority of which the patients would be seen, so on and so forth. The first hour was quiet and loaned itself to chit chat, something, in truth, I have never been comfortable with, nor good. But I figured out quickly, ER nurses had a morbid sense of humor, and once we got past initial pleasantries, the conversation went smoothly.

A couple of sickened elderly patients came through, and they were given plastic ID bracelets and shuffled back to see doctors, as well as a couple of Latino moms, worried and distraught with babies who had terrific coughing fits. Then, a woman came in with her husband helping her as she limped into triage with a protrusion in her sock that turned out to be a shish-kabob skewer she had taken through the foot. It was a surprisingly clean wound that, in retrospect, kind of gives me the willies to think about; after that, the supervising nurse went to the restroom, and I was greeted by an older gentleman, hopping around in pain, wincing, breathing forcefully through his nose. He reported right off the bat he had a pot of frying oil spilled in his lap, and before I could fully register that, he had pulled down his sweatpants to his knees, introducing his red, puffed-up white-blistering genitals. I tried to sound... *clinical* in my observations, noting it looked, well, bad. Second degree burns, certainly. I remembered my mental scorecard and almost cursed my luck, but felt proud that I moved through that nauseating display with poise and professionalism.

The night went on like that, with the only other noteworthy event being a young woman who had some type of tank explosion on the hot dog cart she vended, and she was in rough shape. Grey sheets of skin hung partially off her face like curtains, and she was unbelievably calm, until the nurse went to give her a shot of Demerol; the explosion she was okay with, but the injection, she was not. This seemed puzzling to me, but she was whisked upstairs without too much hesitation to the burn unit, which I had no interest in seeing any further.

I thought about these skills I was learning in class: putting someone in a c-spine position with a suspected neck injury, how to stop an arterial bleed, and I quietly began hoping one of the guys from the halfway house where I was living might get hit by a car, or fall off a road. I was anxious and eager to put these new skills to good practice, and imagined with some clarity my humble response when a passerby would say, "Wow, if it weren't for you, he might have died." To which I would calmly shrug off and explain, "Well, it's a good thing someone knows these things. I was actually kind of busy, but when I saw him in distress, I knew helping out was the right thing to do." My delusional heroics were never to pan out as I hoped, but I still had two more clinical rotations to go, and I was anxious to learn something new.

One of the students in our class - a guy named Pete who sat a couple of desks over — already worked at St. Joseph's Hospital as a tech while he went through the necessary steps to get his EMT before going into nursing. He promised me a good rotation if I went to St. Joseph's on a Saturday afternoon, which usually had a strong storm current of medical emergencies that I could learn a great deal from, so I signed on board for that.

St. Joseph's was a large, red-brick monolithic complex out on the east side by my mom's and had been where I was hospitalized after the second of my two concussions, so I knew it well. Adjoining it was the small Wilmot branch of the public library where I loved to go as a kid. Something about that warm scent of ink and binding glue of new books gave — and still gives — me bright memories of being a child full of wonder and exploration. It was always my favorite place to go when I was much younger.

I passed the library, walking through the maze of squat adjoining medical buildings and gave Pete a call to let him know I was coming. Pete met me in the waiting room of the ER, and used his magnetic key to buzz us back. It was around four o' clock, and the haze was hanging lazily in the sky, beginning to dip below the horizon, and for now, things were pretty quiet.

We sat in the break room working on a small bag of chips we got from the snack machine, and put away a couple of small Styrofoam cups of coffee; I asked Pete if he had ever been to the morgue, out of curiosity, and he stated that he had and that St. Joseph's had one. "Would you like to see it?" he asked, smartly, and I said, "Well, yeah. Of Course."

We went through a maze of antiseptic hallways, past the industrial hum of the massive load washers that took the duty of hospital gowns and towels, past a loading dock, before finally, landing at the morgue in the basement, which required a special keyset to enter. Pete whispered under his breath, "I hate it down here," before gaining entry.

The room was quiet with a funny iodine smell, with large steel drawers on three different walls, with a separate set of shelves with large tea jar looking containers. These contained tumors, fingers, cancerous feet which had been removed, now resting carelessly, bathed in chemicals. I picked one up and looked at the fleshy white tumorous blob that bobbed in the jar, its threat having long since been removed.

Pete opened a drawer and pulled out a yellow and waxy cadaver, its seventy or so years of history fallen silent and lifeless, relegated to a single drawer. Loose and lazy stitching held the chest cavity back together, where whatever drastic surgery had been done to prolong life — in this case — had been unsuccessful. It held no secrets or epiphanies for me, but laid there expressionless, a product of a taken risk that had not panned out.

We moved back through the labyrinth that was the belly of the hospital before taking a service elevator back up, just down the hall from the ambulance entrance, and when we did, a short burst of hell had broken loose. One of the nursing staff I met however briefly when I arrived on shift exclaimed, "Hey, you're the student, right? Follow me, I have something for you." She began to sprint up the hallway in white tennis shoes, her stethoscope barely clutching her neck in doing so.

We were greeted by a racing gurney where the halls intersected, its charge writhing around as two black-clad EMT's flew it down the hall while a third mounted the gurney itself, propped over the patient doing CPR and thrusting violently with both hands to keep the heart beating. A parade of technicians and assistants raced after him as he was brought into the ER and slid onto a prepped table, his life-force jerking about wildly inside him.

I heard one of the paramedics giving the overseeing doctor a full report: his high points being this man had been feverish for days, with some of blood infection having stemmed from an open wound in his foot; patient had a history of substance abuse; patient had been found unresponsive on the bathroom floor with a syringe and a bag of cocaine on the bathroom counter; EMS was called, and life-saving measures were started.

The patient was muscular and, probably otherwise, had a commanding presence, a Latino-American with several gold rope chains and traditional tattoos done in black that let me know, he has been somewhere like the penitentiary, at least once, the kind of guy most people would cross the street over if he had been heading their way. Now, he seemed to be vibrating apart, his eyes rolling back up under their lids, and as soon as he was slid over onto the table, his body seized, his strong forearms jerking about as the nursing staff tried to contain him. The doctor shouted for ten CC's of valium, which were drawn up nearby in what was just a couple of seconds, and injected into his bloodstream, which had little to no effect. The doctor ordered ten more, and the patient twisted up and seized again. Again, no effect. His vitals were taken, and his blood pressure was wildly out of balance as his fevered body crept upwards, boiling from the inside out.

"Temperature!" The doctor called out, to which the nurse replied, "One-oh-five."

"Let's roll the patient on his side," the doctor said, and eight sets of hands rolled him onto one side, and the doctor took a long needle, which looked much more like a *sharpened and malicious straw* and crammed it squarely between a couple of the vertebrae in his back. His spinal fluid was drawn up into the barrel which the doctor, then, held up to the fluorescent light muttered "shit" under his breath, alarmed by what he saw. I would not understand until later the spinal fluid which, also, coats the brain is supposed to be delicate and clear, like that of egg whites freshly cracked open. When it begins to go *white*, it means that like an egg, you have begun to cook, from the inside out. That was the case here.

The doctor looked over at me, as if suddenly aware of my presence, and barked out an order: "You are our student, yes?" he said quickly. "Hold the patients head in place, and hold the jaw open while we intubate." He finished, looking down at the patient who was now panting at a rapid pace, his chest rising and falling in quick shallow breaths as he sprouted sweat from every pour, his flesh having become a troubled fountain, and wildly out of control.

The doctor was talking, and quickly, musing out loud to himself mostly, and he pitched as a greased tube was slid down the patient's windpipe. As soon as it went down, he jerked in discomfort, and I could hear the sound of an unutterable groan as he winced. He began biting at the hose as I heard what sounded like a tooth cracking as his mouth filled up with bile and foam.

"Suction," the doctor said, and a nurse was alongside sucking out the foam and mess with a small, clear tube like you would see at the dentist. The intubation device kicked on, taking over his breathing functions at a slower and more normal rate. No sooner had it been inserted, the whispering hush of the machine coming to life with a hiss, than his body racked with another seizure. From what I was gathering, this was not going well; neither the slowed and controlled breathing nor the flood of calming agents hitting his blood was having any effect. Minutes passed, and I stood there, staring straight down into the patient's eyes as he continued to foam, and the awful sound of teeth cracking against hard vinyl filled up the brief moments of silence while the medical t eam re-grouped.

He had been uttering something for a couple of minutes now, like a mantra, through the girth of the hose as his eyes teared up, and he stared straight up into my face, the same forced half-words, over and over. Curious, I leaned over, *leaned into him,* before I could hear what it was, exactly, he was trying to say. It was "Oh god. Oh god. Oh god."

Oh god.

Suddenly, staring down at his face, my body became light, and I began to pivot on one foot. Like a telescope, blackness crept all around me drawing itself into a tiny circle, a point of light. My knees wobbled. I was going... down. One of the nurses grabbed me, thrusting me back into a chair as another handed me a glass of water. "You.... you ok?" the one asked. I sat there, sheepish, struggling with the fact that against my will, I had begun to faint.

"Yeah, um, yes. I guess so." I managed, getting back to my feet which my knees still pitched a little bit. "I will be." I stood up, and again, not even really knowing that it was still necessary, placed my sweating palms on the patients should blades, though his stifled bark had now become a whisper, and finally, trailed off into nothing. The warm, wet smell of fresh feces filled the emergency room, as the patient let go of his bowels, and his worried stricken look began to change into something else altogether. His taught and tense flesh slid down into rest, at which point the doctor ordered a second round of spinal fluid.

The results told the rest of the story when the thick plastic tube drew up, now, completely white. Something not quite like peace but of utter vacancy washed over the patient's face, and something I have never seen before and could not quite imagine happened: his lips pursed out, his cheeks began to sag, and his hardened and imposing complexion took on the look of what I suppose to be what you would associate as down syndrome. His life held on but his thinking escaped him as I watched before my eyes a grown man turned into a vegetable. The doctor ordered, "Clean him up; give it two hours, then let the family see him." A child's blue blanket, printed with grinning bears holding balloons was wrapped around him, and he was whisked away.

Arriving back to the halfway house late, I was full of doubt and dread, and for the first time, second guessing myself at depth. I hoped to face my own darkness, to work that out somehow in a hospital room, and up to a certain point, felt I had done well in doing so. But watching another man turn to mush in front of me... was unsettling. I slept little, and in the sleep I did get, had dreams of being brain damaged myself, crawling around behind a grocery store as my heart seized. It took me a long time to shake that feeling, like somehow, again, things would take a turn for the worse.

****

"I am so excited," my mother was telling me by phone. "And we are all so, SO proud of you. Your father, too. You are doing great," my mom said, having given her the full report. And the report was I was soon to be let off of probation; I had a good job, however humble, at the Sausage Deli, and I had spoken to the course instructor in EMT about being a volunteer for the Tubac Fire Department, which in my head was a sure thing, less out of self-confidence (which I never had much of) but more out of sheer arrogance than anything. I had reported this to my parents, though, as if I was already hired. And, in truth, in all that had come before, this really was the best I had ever done. Cementing the idea of a bright future sure to come, I had a visit recently by the probation department who applauded me on what looked to be a successful completion of probation, after the past six years or so of going in and out of the courts with no resolution.

Still very much under my mom's long wing, she dutifully took on and helped me with a suitable living arrangement, now that I had an end in sight. I had completed the term agreed to with adult probation, and the correlating halfway house I was ordered to remain at, and functionally, I had stayed sober. On the school front, Hannah, Natalie and myself all got past our course work and completed two intensely regimented written tests and demonstrated our skills with enough competency to take the test from the National Registry of Paramedics, which was set in October. Another guy who I really liked, who always had this great, big smile and wore a fisherman's hat, looked glum when he lifted up his printed grade and saw that he failed the course, but it was that type of course, very unforgiving.

Mom and I went out on a couple of errands and right on the corner of Euclid and Speedway, just a stone's throw away from the University, I found a squat duplex, a mustard yellow older adobe building attached to two other units that I applied for using her as a co-signer, and almost immediately, had come back with a positive result. I was told by the renters it was mine, if I wanted it. My life had turned into something of a stunning victory, and I felt

89

a bright confidence shooting all through me every day of those last two weeks.

Now that my summer semester had finished, I focused on putting in more hours at the deli and began gathering the necessary accruements that would go into making my tiny dwelling a home. Mom bought me dishtowels and an egg pan; matching towels were purchased with a bathmat; a rubbery laundry basket that was on sale was added to the haul.

The halfway house asked me ahead of time if I was open to telling my recovery story to the eighty or so other guys living there on a Wednesday evening, two days before I was slated to move. It was an honor just to be asked.

When the day came, I felt hot fire in my veins as if the world exploded in a vibrant and new color, opening up its door to me to step onto the other side. I already raced out in front of myself deciding I needed something to keep me company, in the way of a ferret, and deciding I would build a wooden shelf dedicated to showing a bunch of small, replica ambulances that I would start collecting as an ode to what I hoped would be a long career. I had all my belongings, the trappings of the new house, stacked in the corner, and I felt borderline heroic having come from so much and overcome so much.

Mom was excited to tell me the most recent news that my sister, Kris, would be returning from San Diego where she moved a year prior. Kris followed her boyfriend Michael out there, who was a timid but sweet soul and who had an opportunity to work in a factory that made a popular brand of skateboards. My sister had done due diligence in finding out what she had to do to transfer out there to teach, but in the meantime was working as a barista with a bunch of co-workers who she never really got along; all reports, thus far, indicated she hated it there in San Diego.

Mom was going to pick her up from the airport; they were going to take me to breakfast mid-morning the following Monday, and I was excited to see Kris again. It was our own celebration of sorts, putting the pain and heartache we had all been through together, behind us.

When Wednesday night came around, I visited the halfway house to tell my story, recounting as best I could my childhood, my wild adolescence, my time — however brief — on the streets in Los Angeles, how I finally came to realize that life was about helping out, which I intently planned to do by way of working up through the ranks of para-medicine. I have always been told I give an eloquent and verbose pitch and have a natural gift to draw people in. I think, even then, this was true, and I got a warm round of applause from my peer group that evening. When my head hit the pillow, I dreamed of great victories to come with the taste of success — however marginal — fresh in my mouth.

THE SHARP END OF THE STICK

FRIDAY, 3:35PM

My new landlords, Tom and Nancy, made sure to meet me in the lot adjoining my new house when I arrived, a set of freshly-made, bright copper keys in hand; the couple was older and extremely thoughtful, proven so by the fact that Nancy baked me a plate of homemade cookies — warm to the touch — as a welcoming gift. Tom unlocked the door for me as we filtered in to the smell of fresh paint and lemon floor cleaner. It was everything I wanted for years — a simple little place to call my own, and I was ecstatic.

Mom picked me up from the halfway house that morning and took me grocery shopping; she helped me unload my first few bags of groceries, and I put them away gingerly. I had just turned twenty-eight, and this would be my first respite from the streets or a lockdown facility in four and a half years. It felt cool and organized and inviting: black and white checkered linoleum lined the kitchen floor until it joined with the panel wood flooring in the main area; an old claw bathtub with bronze feet stood firm in the sizable bathroom; and one wall of the main living area

— interestingly — had wallpaper advertising Coca-Cola, which had its own particular kind of charm. Perhaps most importantly, though, was it felt... *unblemished* by me, by my history and by all I brought to the party. It was as if I had become a living antidote to all things good and wholesome in life, and I had left a heavy footprint everywhere I went. It had been that way for some time. But this was bright and new, full of life.

After making sure I was settled, Tom and Nancy got in their old Lincoln town car in the driveway, and both waved with a cheery smile as they left me to my new place. Mom hung around for a little bit; we both wrestled with putting a new shower curtain in, and she carefully and tactfully helped line up some silverware I bought secondhand in the silverware holder in a drawer — the kind of things doting mothers do when they are propping up their kids for success. Once the surrounding area had the stamp of a mother's approval, she told me, "You've done well. We're so proud of you; Kris will be here, too. She'll be so happy to see you." She said, as if rehearsing the plan to herself. "See you Monday." She kissed me on the cheek and left.

I was *home*. All was well.

I walked around slowly, deliberately, in circles. I opened cupboards, then closed them. I ran my fingers along the wallpaper, opened a window and sat on the small folding futon couch gifted me, letting a fall breeze float in and brush across my face. I sat for a minute, got up, and closed the window. I looked out the window for a while, then, sat back on the couch. I kept going back to the fridge, looking at the same small handful of items I purchased, even though I did not feel hungry in the slightest, as if to make sure they were still there. The more I tried to be *still* and enjoy what I had, the more restless I became. I did not have a TV, well not yet, so I could not distract myself in that way. I felt amazing... yet somehow, I did not. Night fell and sleep evaded me nearly altogether.

Karen, the probation officer assigned to me for field work, surveillance as it were, dropped by late in the afternoon. In her usual style, she wore a heavy, flak jacket with a police radio tucked away into one of the pockets. She wore her hair in a crew-cut, the style that gives away sexual preference, and thin wire horned glasses. As far as folks went, she was a good person and had always been tough on me, but fair.

I had been meticulously arranging details through the day, making sure a bar of soap was lined up on the soap holder *just so,* putting the few odds and ends I had that held any value whatsoever lined up on a shelf, tiny unbroken mementos from a life that had gone less than great, when Karen stopped by.

She walked around half admiring the place, but also just "checking things" which surely was part of her job description, and offered me a congratulations on how things were working out. She told me both she and Ray had serious doubts over the past several years about my outcome, both were in admiration of just how far I had come. The bonus was, after the past six years, my paperwork was "now in the basket" to be released from probation, and I could expect a resolution as soon as that Wednesday. Soon, I would be done. *I would be free.*

6:48PM

I sat, again fidgeting, having arranged and rearranged almost everything in an endless loop like a racecar doing a victory lap that goes on forever, unaware of when to shut it down and let the car and the lap go. Normally, I would have listened to all my favorite songs to christen the moment internally, cement it in some way, but I had not felt like doing that. Since I got there, I could not tell *what exactly* I *did* feel like doing.

A drink to celebrate!

When this thought arrived, it mailed itself in without foreboding: a warm invitation to a glass with ice, filled up half mast with something amber and strong. I bit my lip a little bit, but — in agreement — knew for certain that somehow, this was appropriate. I threw on a light jacket and some Converse and locked my door behind me for the first time, stepping down the street in the warm, electric air. I took 4TH Avenue, with its nightly activities just perking and yawning into life. It took me all of twenty-five minutes to walk to the Double Zero, but I had always been a fast walker.

10:37PM

I had two long island iced teas… okay, three. And a pint of beer. And maybe a three-dollar kamikaze. The mix of spirits settled into my knees and arms, softened my neck, and yet somehow did not quite reach me where I needed it the most. Like many drinks before, the magic and connectivity eluded me; the underlying sense of dread became blurry, but still would not give. It was 11:30pm when an old friend, a musician named Kiko, invited me to an after party. I rode over to Barrio Hollywood, the west side, in the back of a truck. Kiko told me he had some "pretty good pills, three for ten bucks." I told him I only had six. He said, "Good enough."

He told me to start off by only taking half of one, as my knees were starting to buckle and my words slurring. I would not know until some years later, these were "Roche," which were known epidemically as the date rape drug.

I took a half a pill, as he suggested, and all turned to static.

SUNDAY, 8:47AM

I am laying on my black and white checkered floor; its cool and glossy surface pressed against my face with the evaporative cooler whirling in the background. I feel fuzzy and light, and the left side of my body is asleep. I gasp and sit up, bewildered, but recognize quickly, I am at my new home.

I go to the bathroom and splash water on my face and looking back at me is a solemn frown.

I try to stretch and organize myself, my thoughts. I look for my wallet and keys, both of which I find and reach into my pocket to see if I have any stray singles or fives. I do not, but I do pull out cigarette cellophane with two and a half chalky white pills tucked away in it. I go to the toilet, to flush them, and the thought hits me: that would be a waste of six dollars.

I try not to think too much more but take the other half of the pill from last night, hoping it might help me sort myself out.

It does.

11:35AM

A warm and friendly rush takes hold, my limbs careless and loose, my head a warm pot of oatmeal. My worries and cares slide gently away, the confusion of the morning now placed squarely on a shelf. This half a pill seems magical, and it inspires plans of every type. Patterns of décor rushing through my head, lots of small things, trinkets, I need to purchase with some immediacy to make this small nest I am building complete. A more-than-strong urge comes over me to call several old friends and profess my deep care for them. The sunshine coming through the window seems perfect for a bike ride on a day like this, a fine idea.

Suddenly, a thought begins to ride solely unaccompanied through my mind, a careless and music-less tune that draws me in: whatever these pills are, surely, they'd be more effective if I inject them. This idea seems a good one.

2:35PM

I decided to go pay my old friend, Doug, a visit. I decided that when I arc my path over to his place, it might be best to cut up the alley and jump over the fence, as Doug lives across the street from the men's home where I had just moved out, and had numerous failures and successes over the past few years. *Yes, a plan that best not to be seen.* I made sure to be careful. I jumped on my bicycle, the pavement disappearing from beneath my tires. The air felt good on my face, the sun a friendly co-pilot. My life felt light and good. I cannot remember when I felt happier.

3:35PM

I made it, undetected. I had some technical difficulties jumping the fence, a few cuts on my ankle but nothing serious. I fell like a sack of potatoes once I got over the top. My friend was happy — albeit surprised — to see me, and me him. I wasted no time asking for what I needed, a syringe, and I was in luck. He had 'one of those' for me. He, also, had heroin he told me. I methodically went about seeking a trade on some level: a white pill, for a little bit —

just a smidgen — of black tar heroin. *Yes. A good idea.* We traded off, and I went into the bathroom, and drew up some water; I sat down on the toilet and went to my ritual I had known many times before. *A tide of narcotic seawater rushes up over my face, and I disappear.*

SUNDAY ??????

I am on a gurney, captured somehow, and men dressed in navy blue are attending me, a sense of motion as I'm being wheeled somewhere, beneath a tree, down a driveway. I see the hue of red lights flickering off the edge of the roof that I roll under. I'm being asked questions to which I don't respond. A panic, a real one begins to steal over me. The last thing I see as I'm loaded into an ambulance is a dozen or so men that I know well, watching from the porch of the Hedrick House as I am loaded up. They stand there quietly, and I try not to make eye contact, but I already have. I am loaded up as the legs on the gurney slam with a clack, then we rocket off up the street, sirens blaring.

I am wheeled through a maze of white hallways; I am hooked up to a heart monitor. The medication I am given to "block" the heroin is only partially effective, and I am asked what else did I take? What was it? I withhold information. A police officer comes in, my driver's license in his hands, and he asks me questions. Again, I say nothing. I raise my hand to try to swipe my driver's license back, and my limbs function but all too slowly. He leaves the room. I am not handcuffed to the bed. I get up to leave, and I run — or more like lumber — out. I am in the cool night of the desert in shorts and a gown, and I head up First Avenue, just a couple of miles, but it feels like forever, but perhaps, I won't remember this later, only I've fallen, my hands, knees and forehead now scraped. Just a guy in a hospital gown, despondent, on his way home. It raises no concern of any passerby.

I sleep, not far from the door.

The kitchen floor feels cool to the touch, and good.

MONDAY, 9:35AM

My cell phone is ringing; I think it has been ringing, maybe a few times, dragging me into consciousness. Over and over, ringing. I prop myself up on the counter, and answer in a hoarse voice. It is the lady I work for at the Sausage Deli. She tells me I was supposed to have come in early, and place an order, and asks me where I am. (I don't remember what I said, but it was a brief call.) Playground-like childhood scrapes mark me up, and the hospital gown hangs off me like a tragic and failing curtain. I splash water on my face, and there is a knock? At the door? I attempt to recalibrate, force myself into composure, feeling awful. Thinking, and trying very hard, not to. I throw on a t-shirt and answer the door.

"Hey, you!" my sister greets me, as she throws her arms around me, adding, "Well! Let's see the new place!"

Her look of excitement turns to a puzzled look, then a mild frown.

"Are you alright?!" she asks, standing quiet in the doorway, mother hovering in the background.

"Yes, totally, fine…um, yes. Just fine." I croak, ushering them in the door as somewhere in the background the sound of more tires crunching on gravel fills my ears. I go to close the door, and it snaps back, partially opened now by another hand on the other side. I see Ray; I see Karen, and two uniformed officers behind them, the door pushes open. Panic sets in. I struggle a bit, pulling away, dazed and pulling back from what I created, but I am shoved hard into a wall and cuffed.

My family asks questions through their sobs that are, now, inescapable. I am whisked to the back on an unmarked car, and a firm hand on my shoulder pushes me inside. I can't hear now, only see.

I stare out the back window, and my mother and sister in tears on the porch, my mother clutching a small, wrapped housewarming gift in her hands. Something deep inside me bends… then snaps. I wish — more than ever before — I could disappear. The car rolls out of the driveway, as the only two women I have ever had in my life, grow smaller and smaller in the rear windshield.

"I'm sorry," I whisper to no one. Then, I go crazy.

BREATHING APPARATUS

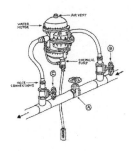

It is Halloween; I am being released from jail after thirty or so days. With a swipe of a gavel, I hear I am, now, a convicted felon: any chance I had of having my history erased is, now, forlorn. But I am free to go; at twenty-eight years old, and for the first time in a long time, I am free. Nobody picks me up, but I did not call anyone to ask. I walk home in the same t-shirt and shorts I was in a month earlier. Inexplicably, I still have my house keys in my pocket, so I let myself in, and that tiny, wrapped housewarming gift sits on the counter, but I cannot open it. I walk to the Korean-owned mart around the corner, and buy a bottle of Wild Irish Rose, which hits me warm and fast, but I have this feeling that something is deeply wrong, a tight spring in my chest unyielding to this self-talk assuring myself that things will work out okay because they usually do not.

This feeling has been here ever since that Monday morning, a living puzzle inside me, somehow, I cannot assemble. I meant to do well; I meant to stay sober. Somehow in a matter of hours, on the finest day I have ever known, I reached deep into the jaws of victory to pull out a stunning defeat. It feels like nails in my head thinking about it, and I cannot shake it.

In all this consternation, a simple relief of not having to run, or hide, settles. I am free — for now — to do as I please. It occurs to me — in a deep and serious way — to get in touch with a community somewhere that helped guys like me get on track, people that help other people get sober. I've known many. This seems like a fine idea.

Two weeks, I think; that is exactly how much time I need, and that is when I will re-seek some version of help, in two weeks.

I am sitting on my sliver of a porch, which was really a sidewalk that faced four busy lanes of traffic, finishing this bottle of wine, when an old acquaintance who we all knew as Jonny Trouble rides up on a bike. He sits with me and tells me he has a bag of methamphetamine in his pocket, which I have not done in years, literally.

I am still entertaining the thought of an imaginary timetable of when I will fix my life while we take flight; the nasty, yellow powder working its magic as my teeth start to grind.

My thought of seeking out help, somehow, is now replaced by a new thought. Maybe this stemmed from defeat, maybe the wine; maybe it is a tincture of all of them combined. But a new thought cuts through my head like a bullet, replacing that thought with a foreboding and certainty to it… a finality to it.

*I never want to be sober, ever, **ever**, again.*

****

It was not so long after I talked to my sister by phone who — deciding San Diego was not for her — moved back to Tucson and had resumed duties at this place called Cappuccino where she had been employed off and on for years. Feeling bad for me, and like she might be able to do something to help, she coerced management into giving me an opportunity for a job, making sandwiches a few days a week on the evening shift. Being mostly a coffee hang out, on a busy evening, it might total only about twenty sandwiches. Easy enough, and no pressure. The only drawback to that was it was *me* they were asking.

The night preceding my interview was one of some heavy drinking. I woke up — per the norm — around one-thirty, which was plenty of time to make my 3:00pm job interview. It was a particularly hot day, but I decided to ride my bicycle the three or so miles, in hopes of being hired. A third of the way there, I rode over a piece of glass, and with a quick hiss, my front tire deflated itself, lifeless.

I thought it was an idea to take my bike and place it on the bus rack on the front, and take the bus to the interview. I was right in the middle of being between bus stops, and squinting into the distance, I could see the silhouette of a bus approaching. I ran for the nearer stop, pushing the bike with its flat tire, and fortunately, I make it, beet-red, sweating and panting. I saw the bus slow down to pick me up when my stomach went into a heavy churn, did a couple of back flips, and emptied itself all over the sidewalk. The bus slowed, and I saw the driver shaking his head, speed up again, and was gone. I walked the remainder of the way, pushing my bike. I showed up a sickeningly shade of yellow and bright red with vomit on my shirt, fifteen minutes late. I was told, "It's okay. Why don't we try again tomorrow," discharged of my duties to answer questions to obtain employment.

The interview went well, but during all that, I slid into some sort of depression, the kind I always got before, like depression with an *edge* to it. My remedy was a large bottle of tequila, the kind with the handle on the side to carry the girth of the treasure it contains. "My first day of the job, I will start working on it," I tell myself as I reached a screaming low and contemplating the essence of life itself. I would, also, head over to a new acquaintance of mine, a guy named Malcolm who had a shlock of curly hair and a house rich with fauna and plants in every corner, hanging everywhere. Malcolm had flamingo neon lights in his home and a hot tub in the living room. Malcolm dealt crystal meth. With a warm flood of tequila that hit my senses, I went to Malcolm's; he was quick to sell me something, and asked if I might be alright with giving another girl sitting in his living room a place to stay. Her name was Kim, a tall and vivacious brunette, who will — later that evening — tell me she just turned state's evidence on a few people and was trying to get into the witness protection program.

We ended up driving over to my house in her small pick-up, the contents of her life scattered in the back in garbage bags and cheap baskets. I did not know it then, but our one and only week together was about to get interesting.

It was Kim's second day staying with me, and she invited over an old friend of hers, this older man, Jim, who has muscular dystrophy. His limbs moved wildly about like jello, his neck and wrists bobbed and weaved in cobra-like fashion as he placed — from his shaking hands — a large pile of powdered crank on a small CD case, inviting us to partake. Kim snorted a noxious line up each nostril, and I did the drugs in my own fashion, quickly and almost immediately feeling the effects of cotton fever come on, having gotten something in my bloodstream. My muscles began to twitch and ache, and I threw up in the kitchen sink a handful of times. I started shivering, my teeth clacked in rhythm and she ran me a hot tub, for lack of anything else to do. I tripped on a wet towel sitting on the bathroom floor and went down. I smacked the edge of the cast iron tub with my mouth and heard plastic snapping as my partial dentures were annihilated. Blood poured from my mouth, as I have bitten my tongue. I sat there shivering in the tub before remembering, I was supposed to be on shift.

I called — and with some efficiency — to let them know I knocked out my teeth and would not make it in to work. My flesh bucked like a rodeo animal for a good bit before I eventually settled down and fell mercifully into sleep.

The next day, both alcohol and drugs flew freely, but on that day, it seemed to be the alcohol I mostly focused on, as the tequila rose to my head. Kim and I went out in the morning to respond to an ad in the newspaper, and I got a new kitten. I named him Elvis, and we brought him home where I returned to drinking. Around the seventh drink, Kim told me that a drug dealer was holding most of her clothes hostage, as she owed him forty dollars; and three drinks later, a fresh burst of bravado suggested that we shall go and get those clothes back, post haste.

I was quite drunk as we piled in her small pick-up to drive over to a small house with a high fence around it, and an off-brand of small electronic cameras on the fence's perimeter, electronically gazing at us, and we rang the jerry-rigged doorbell. The wooden gate opened and a man in overalls was standing there, pointing a crossbow at my head. We exchanged words, but in forty minutes time, we had all become the best of friends, and sat around a coffee table drinking, telling stories, and getting high. Kim got her clothes back, and I suddenly realized, "I am to be late for work, again." I called — matter-of-factly — explaining I had an incident, though I could not tell them too much, other than a crossbow was involved, and I needed to take the evening off.

The next morning, Kim departed for Flagstaff to see her parents and lay low for a while. Though I did not know it yet, I would not see her again for many years, when she would be doing much better, as would I.

The morning she left, I stood in the front yard in socks, boxer shorts and a sleeveless t-shirt waving goodbye; we had a fine time, she and I, and almost immediately, I sunk into a deep and profound depression. I went inside and took a drink; the handle of tequila I bought got much, much lower in quantity but still had enough left to work its magic.

Somewhere along in the way, I got an old couch, a faded red velvet throwback from the sixties that I did not have adequate space for inside, so I decided to put on the porch. Being a high traffic area on a major street, I hung a small, cardboard sign in the window where the couch rested, exclaiming, 'DO NOT SLEEP HERE HOMELESS PEOPLE!' So I was a little surprised in the late afternoon to open my front door to get the mail and see an older gentleman, eccentrically dressed, sitting back with his head resting in his hands, eyes closed, on my couch. I gave him a tap on the shoulder and pointed to the sign. "Hey buddy," I said as he startled awake. "It says no homeless guys can sit here. Ya gotta go."

He exclaimed rather quickly that he was not homeless: he was a college professor at the university. "Interesting." I said, rubbing my chin thoughtfully. "Would you like to come in and have some drinks with me?" He agreed this was a fine idea and stepping inside was greeted with a plastic cup half full of tequila. He fished through a battered old briefcase and pulled out what appeared to be a large manuscript. It was, he said, his life's work, a dissertation on weather patterns in the South Pacific, or something like that. He asked me if he might read me what he felt were its finest elements, and I agreed. He read aloud, and we worked off what was left in the large, glass bottle before reality faded out altogether.

****

I awake with a course cough, and the curious sense that I am choking. I cough and cough, and my eyes burn when I open them. I have no idea where I am, or what is happening. I trip and nearly fall, bumping into walls, feeling for a light switch, stumbling down a hall. Everything seems unusually dark, and I have no idea why my lungs feel hot. I have no idea why I cannot stop coughing.

I fumble through what feels like a hallway, and see a bright outline of an orange square floating in the darkness. I stare at it curiously, not knowing what it means. I continue to cough, and starting to panic, scream for help. I soon discover I passed out and left a potpie in the oven, set to broil mistakenly. The drywall and wallpaper behind the old stove are beginning to ignite, and nasty, dark brown stains streak all the way to the celling. My neighbor, Ryan, hears me call for help. Rather than use the adjoining door, he throws a brick through the kitchen window. He gets a garden hose and douses the whole mess. By the time I find the light switch, the house is full of dense, grey smoke; water is everywhere, and one wall of the house is pretty much ruined. The smell hangs around well into the next morning, when I awaken and realize, I'm late for work. It's okay though; I call and explain there has been a house fire, not too much damage, but I will need to investigate some things, and let them know I will see them tomorrow.

****

My next employment would fare none too better. I got a kitchen job at a popular eatery and brewery on the university campus. On day two, carrying a giant stack of dinner plates with several razor-sharp chef's knives on top, I stepped in a small oil slick on the kitchen floor, and down I went. When I stood up, my left forefinger was cut in between the knuckle, nearly severing it, tendon and all. They were understanding: accidents happen. They were far less understanding after a workman's compensation was filed, and the results of my drug screen came back. I remember the bewildered look on the general manager's face when he told me I dropped dirty for *everything.* I shrugged my shoulders before retorting, "It has been a pretty interesting week..."

After that, I would not know any real employment for quite some time. My brain became an addled and disorganized mess. Other means of self-destruction presented themselves along the way, and as a result, I found myself on the methadone program, driving my bicycle a few miles every morning to a clinic for a quick cherry-flavored morning narcotic, which became my version of a strong cup of coffee.

As a result of spending more time at Malcolm's, a whole host of interesting characters began to worm themselves into my life, mostly at my own invitation to do so. I grew strangely dim to an odd sense I always had, a deep internal caution, a warning sign, which rather than heed, I simply learned to drink through. Whenever I felt uncomfortable or felt like something was about to end very badly, I would just drink more. And I hoped, *maybe this will go away.*

I remember one particular day having that feeling, more so than any time in my twenty-eight years, which I curtly ignored. A guy — Chris — I knew but maybe two weeks, asked a question, one he felt I might benefit. "Hey Jeff, do you think my brother, Tony, can **cook here?**"

I was not exactly sure what he meant, though I had a hunch, so I asked him to elaborate. He told me, "You know, *cook.* Speed. He is driving around with a lab in the trunk of his car, and has no place to set up shop, no place to try to make money." Then, he told me, "You get twenty-five percent of everything he is to make." My guts were a squirming basket of eels, and the hair on the back of my neck stood on end as I considered that proposition thoughtfully. I finished the rest of my beer in nearly one swallow.

"Yeah, sure. Let's do it..."

The first time I met Tony, it was just for a minute; I gave him the key to my small house and told him to "do his thing" and that I would be back in the morning to collect my percentage. In truth, I was terrified of my house exploding, of something going wrong; my guts were in knots, and again, I tried to just drink through it.

When I came back in the mornings from having stayed at my mom's, my house had not turned into smoldering ash; and to my amazement, I had not been robbed. Tony hung around waiting for me to get back; hell, he even bought us breakfast burritos once. After we ate and had a little coffee, he said, almost as an afterthought, "Oh yeah, this is for you." He reached in his pocket and pulled out a sandwich bag with a hefty handful of a shiny, pinkish crystals in it. My curiosity got the better of me, and I asked him if he wanted to come back next week, knowing next time around, I would like to stay...

A week later, Tony showed back up. A little bit after dark, he parked his car so the rear of it faced the back door, and he brought in several plastic tubs: big Pyrex vessels and lots of plastic hosing; denatured alcohol and brake cleaner for cars; a small sandwich bag full of a brick red powder, red phosphorus (which I later found out was the most difficult ingredient to get); and muriatic acid.

Tony began to talk, to tell me his trade secrets. He shared about coming from a county in southern California where he learned his craft from one in a group he dubbed "the magnificent seven." All were journeyman drug manufacturers that started producing drugs in their homes decades before.

He talked for hours, often, using the word Cook — not as a verb but as a proper noun — a name he had given this thing he did that he spoke of fondly:

"Every Cook has its own personality, its own way of being, man. Sometimes your Cook wants to resist you, a slow starter. You just need to coax it out sometimes, man. Talk to it; heat it up; it will go. Other times, your Cook goes hot, wants to blow on you, wants to get out of control and get in your face. I've had it happen once..."

He was staring off into space, rubbing his chin hair.

"This one, yeah one time, it blew on me, right off the jump. It was *pissed,* too. My beaker shattered, and the Cook got out. This purple cloud of smoke, it attacked me. Followed me around the house and chased me into the front yard. It wanted to get me, but you know what? I got it, man. *I got it!* I got a garden hose and sprayed at it. I told it, 'Fuck you, Cook.' Then, it went up the street and disappeared. It was gone."

I will never be sure if I believed him or not, with his wildly superstitious ideas and suppositions but one thing I knew for sure. I knew *he* believed every word of what he said.

He showed me everything he knew, and we quickly became friends: I, the understudy, and he, the teacher. We would stay up and experiment with chemicals all night, tightly taping down hoses, creating poisonous gases out of foil and acids, doing our thing. And when we unlocked the doors in the morning, after splitting molecules all night, I felt a strange buzzing all through my limbs, like walking away from a nuclear power plant. It was a strange and peculiar time...

Outside of his felonious past and present, I found Tony to be both incredibly creative, and likable. We would cross paths about seven years later, and I would help him make a beginning at getting sober.

Stretching through those months, my world seemed to take on new and odd proportions that only those that have shed the habit of sleep would truly understand. The sky yawned awake and kissed me goodnight like clockwork as days rolled in and out like the tide, and every day was a new and strange adventure. I have seen people — plenty of them — that did not have the stomach for this; some would eventually run down the street screaming bloody murder, delirious and terrified, but I found — inexplicably — I had a strong constitution for this. I had a curious fascination with the hallucinations that came from sleep deprivation: they did not scare me; they interested me. And with it came a sense of invincibility, with some admitted unwanted side effects. In the midst of that toxic environment, I found myself shedding off fingernails and toenails like something from a horror film, which forced me to reason, I was sure I was turning into something ... *incredible*, like from the movie 'The Fly.' One of my newfound associates told me he thought we could change our own natural pH levels and become immune to cancer. I loved the idea of that.

A few weeks later, I started driving a taxi as a side way to make some extra money. In actuality, that was not true: I started doing it so I would have a car on loan to me in the hopes of making connection in organized crime where I could whisk crime bosses about with whatever it was they needed, and earn my right to take home a car in doing so. I was operating from the unfounded supposition that I had *never* seen a cab pulled over and assumed that they must not get pulled over, which seemed to make my idea a good one. I took the time to print up my own business cards, which stated 'Iconoclastic Taxi Courier,' with a picture of a little bubble space car on it, like from the kids show 'The Jetsons.' I did not really know what iconoclastic meant, but it sounded cool. I felt proud with that business card. Only important people had those, and I was one of them.

Of course, I was never really sober when I drove, and would either fill the bandwidth of the car with mindless chatter to passengers who looked generally quite relieved to be dropped off, or sometimes I would simply park and lose consciousness for a good amount of hours, the static of the CB radio still crackling to life when I re-emerged. And in the middle of all that was Elvis, my black and white cat with a small litterbox and food and water dish on the floor of the front seat. At least one time, a passenger objected with, "But I'm allergic to cats."

"Well, call a different cab then," I said, roaring off.

My other 'work,' as it were, was acquiring things for a man named Jack. I met him through Tony, and he was up to the same types of activities, but on a much bigger level. He would send me on these fantastic errands to get boxes and boxes of cold medication, and sometimes car parts or power tools. Jack got cancer in his face, and had already had one ear removed, and half of his nose was to be removed surgically when I met him. But I did not think he was living a lifestyle conducive to following medical advice, so I do not know that he ever went back; I think he just let the cancer kill him. His wife, Pam, was covered in baggy skin and long scars across all four limbs. She claimed to have been kidnapped by the government and kept as their property in a series of weight loss experiments. The evidence seemed to support that, but I never knew, like Tony, if I believed her or not. But I knew that she believed it.

I would run errands for Jack every day, and I was a good steward of the responsibilities given me, except for the times I was not. Those times, he would scream at me in a Cajun unintelligible drawl, and I never knew what he said, only that he was pissed.

A parade of assorted characters had infiltrated my life, of course at the prompting of my own invitation. In naivety, I imagined myself as being part of a world where the essence of being at the epicenter of "the party" rang true. Of course, sometimes certain people would go around with dark pathologies and offer to sell silencers or chloroform. When I did sleep, again, I found myself in a world filled with nightmares, and the prickling of the hair on the back of my neck became constant around my newfound associates. I was keeping company with the devil himself...

My life as a taxi driver was short lived, as I was always in trouble with the office, saying inappropriate things over the CB radio in an impaired state, or simply coming up short on the funds to keep renting the car in twelve-hour shifts, which became expensive. My tired and worried mother would dutifully show up with two sacks of groceries every week and a rent check once a month, as I had all but shucked any responsibility to leading and living a normal life. It was around that time, as my health deteriorated, that one morning after having been awake for almost a week, I found myself a passenger in her car, driving down the road with the FM radio on. A newsflash cracked through the soft-rock station my mom would ordinarily listen to, stating there were early reports that a plane had hit a building in New York City, the World Trade Center as it were. Unalarmed, I drew a simple portrait in my head of a small, prop airplane glancing across the side of a giant tower, clipping a fax machine and breaking a typewriter as it did so. It was not until I got home and turned on the television that the horror of that day swallowed me whole. Quite a thing to digest in that state.

I think I sensed — somewhat dimly — all along that the free ride, with its special narcotic cup of methadone every day, the free rent and groceries, the endless hours to do exactly as I pleased, and the endless free supply of drugs for the taking, could not last forever. The golden days of being insane and carefree had always, in some sense, seemed 'too good to be true,' for whatever that meant. And despite it, change was the furthest thing from my mind. Much like a house cat, my eyes adapted to the darkness around me and made the best of what I had been given.

But in October 2002, the few sole things for which I held a deep affection started to go. I was courting a woman named Raina who — while interested in growing alongside me — was told through a friend-of-a-friend all that I was up to and had given me an ultimatum. It was one that I found myself utterly unable to commit, though I would have liked to, and off she went away for good; I was crushed.

Two days later, little Elvis, the black and white spotted kitten I got the year before, was struck in the road, breaking his rear legs. My next-door neighbor, Ryan, tried to be helpful and said he was willing to take the cat into the desert to put it down, but I could not do that. My parents loaned me the money to put him down, and a void beyond anything I had felt up to that point overtook me. I had not cried that hard in years.

I began to ramp up my own operation, taking all I learned from both Jack and Tony, with almost zero results. This craft I thought I knew so well had eluded me, and I would usually end up with a jar full of toxic liquid chemicals that would kill anything that might ingest it, yet I was obsessed with the process. My mind whirled with measurements and possibility, scraping matchbooks by night to get enough phosphorous to give it another try.

One day, a guy I met on the streets named Matt was over, and we were trying to do a small batch of something. I preheated my element, and a small pot of vegetable oil on top of it to control the temperature of my cook. I decided to wait for the oil to come to a boil, and then back it off for a while, before beginning. The pan did not seem to want to come to a boil, and in that delirious state, I made an incredibly dangerous oversight. Taping my hose down tightly, I submerged the glass beaker in the pan of oil, not recognizing it already shot up well over five hundred degrees. The glass went white hot, and began to crack almost immediately. Dark and colorful gases filled the hoses in seconds as the angry, black concoction roared to life. I pulled it out of the oil, but it was too late. The glass shattered in my hands, and I took a deep breath full of that glowing gas. As the emergency wound down, the chemicals settling into an ooze of broken glass on the counter, a deep and profound exhaustion over took me. I laid down on the bed and faded out in seconds. I think I remember waking up and having only black and white vision for a few moments, before falling out again, and this time, for the entire night.

In the aftermath of Elvis, I decided to get a pet mouse. I think I saw a movie somewhere in which one of the side characters always had a mouse in his pocket; it seemed artsy and I thought it might add eccentricity to my persona. Upon purchasing one, I found out right away, it did not care much for staying put in my pocket, and probably did not care too much for me either. It got away from me in my first hour of bringing it home, and when I looked for it an hour later, it was dead in the closet. The fumes in my home had not been hospitable to the fragility of a smaller life.

I heard somewhere about the heroin trade in New York. That block-by-block in the more hardscrabble parts of the inner city, one could walk up to an old tenement building where a bucket would be lowered from an upper story window, and you could place your ten dollars in it, and a bag of heroin would be lowered moment later. But the thing that held my interest was each separate dealer had *named* their product, things like Scorpion, Body Bag, or Turbo. It was the only means of discernment the buyer had to know who had something really good on any given week, and the system operated on the same principles as the stock market. If, say, Turbo was known to have caused a few overdoses in a week, it was presumed that batch of heroin had not been cut much and street-level users would flock to that street, looking to maximize their dollar.

I liked that, the idea of a name, a brand, my thing, all my own, that I could create and be noted for… only, my results were nothing salable by any means. However, that did not stop me from talking myself up as some underworld entrepreneur. "We're going to take this town by a STORM," I remember telling a guy I knew over the phone, then added, "Just you wait and see."

Some weeks prior to this, there were a few folks in town who were only known as the Phoenix People, at least by the folks I knew who knew them. They were bikers, cooks, nefarious types coming down to look at doing business somehow in Tucson. I never met them, only heard they were there. A week or so later, somebody I knew said, "The Phoenix People are cutting out, leaving town. They have an inside guy, inside the department, says shit is going down man. Bigtime."

I got so sick of everyone's cloak and dagger bullshit: the endless ramblings of the paranoid and the spooked, thinking wires were in the walls and secret wiretaps lay everywhere. I did not believe a single word of it and did not give it any credit when people told me — in fact, multiple times — that I was being watched.

Turned out, they were correct.

I could have never imagined how right they turned out to be.

NOVEMBER 27, 2002: 6:35AM

It was odd how I never heard the storm outside converging and creeping up closer and closer. For what had come was a hunter with its prey fixated in sight. I say this — about being none the wiser — only because at that time, two different windows in my home were broken, letting in outside flies and the sounds of traffic and passersby. My home matched what had become, overall, a tattered and toxic environment: the claw bathtub I tried to paint black ruined; what had once been a keen and appealing checkered linoleum floor was covered in purple iodine stains; and the entire place smelled like an oil refinery with a noxious chemical odor that no longer yielded to household cleaners or incense to cover up.

Equally odd was the sound of the helicopter circling overhead that, also, went unnoticed. I was embroiled, again, in the process: a glass beaker in front of me beginning to heat up, and laying out my plans carefully, when I heard bellowing from the door.

"POLICE! SEARCH WARRANT!"

The door exploded inward in a swift motion, the light of the morning peeking through a flood of police that poured in the door —bullet proof vests, helmets, and ski masks covering their faces. One thick palm grabbed my neck, and I was hurled to the floor, my forehead bouncing off it. A sense of alarm grabbed the room as the arresting party had not actually expected any manufacturing to be taking place when they arrived, and care was taken immediately to gently shut everything down. I laid there on the floor, a boot on my neck, watching the red dots of laser sighting from their weapons dance around the kitchen wall in a crazy pattern.

The picture rail that encircled the entirety of the house had been lined with hundreds of fortified wine bottles, mostly MD 20/20 which began to tumble and shatter on the floor as the maelstrom continued; every shelf, every drawer was cast about in an aggressive search for something more as I laid there, my thoughts whirling.

I was pushed over on my back as a uniformed officer began to cut off my clothes with box cutter; covered in iodine stains, they were collected as evidence. I was pulled to my feet, my hands zip-tied tightly behind my back, stark naked. In front of — who I, later, find out was — MANTIS Narcotics Squad, and male and female personnel both.

I stood there as a great shame stole over me, such as I had never known. I felt fit for crucifixion. Mixed with that was another sense I had never felt before; it was the sense of any real hope, somewhere deep tucked inside my humanity, circling down a drain, a hollow certainty that my life was simply **over** had come. Not with tears or a defeated shriek, just a quiet recognition.

****

I am being questioned now, seated in the front seat of a silver paneled truck which I believe to be a mobile testing laboratory. Nearby, a parked tank-like armored vehicle sits, and the entire block is locked down with a dizzying display of patrol car lights. Tape is being strung in every direction in the background; a Spanish speaking Mexican news crew just arrived and are filming live. A few of the words they are saying, I pick up.

Unable to comprehend my situation, I turn to my captor, looking for sympathy, perhaps comfort by the person nearest me, grasping for something, anything, to lessen the shock to my system.

"So…" I start, "Is this… I mean, is this, like, a really big deal? Do you think I'll be okay?" I ask, as he begins to hammer away with questions. (I found that strange, looking back, that I sought comfort there.)

He smirks and laughs in my face, "Eight-to-twenty, asshole."

Eight to twenty… Years!

The words in his inquiry contain the word pounds. "Where are the pounds?! You have ten pounds or more, we know you do! You have ten thousand dollars, we know that, also. We know it. Where is it? Where did you get the red? Who distributes for you? Are you going to cooperate, or should we rip this place to pieces?"

I respond that they have the wrong guy, and the wrong idea; to this point, I am correct. I have seven dollars and am caught with no methamphetamine. What I had been working on hadn't "turned" yet (which proved to be a great blessing).

One of the other officers points to the tiny guest house just behind mine, and figures it must be the stash house, where I keep all "the goods." A small mechanical spider-like device is used, and the lock is instantly blown apart and mangled. A terrified neighbor sits up in bed, and yells for help. They calm him down, and he comes to join the spectacle.

Soon, I am dressed in a chemical suit that feels like rice paper, a flimsy white thing that zips up the front. Tom and Nancy, my landlords arrive and stand there, shaking their heads. The neighbors, also, stand there, watching, asking questions. From the corner of my eye, I see crates and trunks of my belongings being hauled out of the house as the paper mache artwork I worked so hard to create is trampled into dust in the doorway.

I am brought back to the concrete monolith where I have been housed many times before.

This time, it swallows me whole.

DOWN IN THE WELL

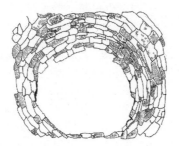

There are parts of this story that may seem improbable I suspect, and I recognize — even as the author — that because the tale itself, from beginning to end, is sometimes hard for me to believe. Every now and then, I wake up with the small, warm bodies of my pets sniffing my face, wrapped up in a clean and cozy blanket, and I marvel at the simplicity of a healed mind and a life in bloom on the other side of it. In person, I do, at times, like to stretch a tale, usually for comedic value. But for the purposes of this writing, I have checked and re-checked, and made an appraisal to share with the reader some basic facts, plain and simple; along with some remedies I found that have become a foundation of sorts, a path to wellness. As I mentioned before, other parts of that path have been omitted altogether, things that have proved to be a great panacea which are best kept personal.

It has been my living experience to discount myself, often writing things off altogether, as if I had no value and was not worth the time of day. I mentioned earlier, after my second concussion, in the middle of the most tragic emergency of my life up to that point, the only thing I could think of was to apologize for bleeding on that clean, white carpet, as if nothing else mattered at all. In my soul, that set up a pattern; somewhere, deep down in the well, I always felt as if me just existing required an apology, to whom, I was never sure. Through a process of deep self-examination, I have been able to hold some things, such as that, up to the light. I know, now, why, after being rear-ended in my car, I told the other driver, "Just give me twenty bucks, man. It's cool." My life played out from that basis, a Walking Apology maybe washing dishes for a meager wage, or riding a bus. And needing to apologize for all of it: for living, for breathing, for being alive.

I began my teenage years with a dark secret that I kept well concealed, well below the surface. A quiet, little truth between me and myself, never to be held up for public examination. My thinking, as it were, had *changed,* **drastically** so, an unexpected jaunt down into a dark well, where uglier things breathed, lurked, wrapping themselves up in my thoughts, painting grotesque *visions* in my mind's eye, things I did not want to think about or ruminate on, yet, there they were. Though, eventually, I adapted, there was a suddenness to the beginning of all that that alarmed me. It is quite a thing for the sunshine of childhood to go into eclipse, another for the sun never to return. I have a friend David in Los Angeles that once made mention that on some level, we are like cats: our eyes simply adjust to the darkness after a time.

But the secret that I am referring to was became a malevolent and growing violence inside me. I think, on some level, I have the soul of a pacifist; I abhor cruelty and violence; it makes the hairs on my neck stand up, and I squirm in the presence of it. There were some years where I fancied myself a 'street tough,' but that never exactly measured up to who I have ever truly been. This, of course, created great difficulty when at an earlier season in my life, having been knocked in the head severely, more than once, my thought-life became overflowing with dark and scary content — the bells of a lower level of hell ringing clear through my thoughts. A door opened, and I never knew how to shut it. I only knew — or thought I knew — if I were to talk about my dark secret, it would not be well received. And, in truth, it most likely would not have been. The science of thought patterns and the prognosis of that is but in its infancy. If you talk about murdering people or hurting animals — even if you had not nor even wanted to — well, that is still be a bad thing. I knew that as fact, even as a young boy.

If I could change anything about that very early time, the suffering consequence from having a brain injury, I think I wish I would have found some type of working faith much earlier — be it real or imagined — a higher shelf onto which to place my troubles and cling to for the sake of being okay. But that was never to be. My homeostasis, as it were, went over a cliff before it had even fully developed. I dreamed of and thought of typhoons of razor blades tearing me to pieces, or dead factories full of squirming things with doors that would not open. I questioned my sanity early on, as young as fourteen, and many times later to close friends in my twenties.

As mentioned, I discounted all of that. Whatever changed inside me was not important enough to mention, even when the shroud of secrecy faded, because, beneath it, I thought I did not matter.

One of the platitudes which I rested, and maybe one that had not served me was the bootstrap mentality that goes like this: "It is what it is; whatever happened, happened; move on." And, whilst there is a resilience embedded in the emboldening of the spirit, this lacks any depth, any insight, and therefore, contains no answers.

In truth, even decades later, having been prone to frightful thoughts — on occasion — that veered out of my control, (even now) I dismissed them. Hence, it is merely a matter of both circumstance and coincidence that this book was ever written. I have come across several people — both personally and professionally — who have, also, suffered head injuries, and had taken a keen interest in how that all worked; and they found a great deal of identification as a result, and in that identification, I found answers to questions that stretched back nearly thirty years. It is quite a thing to know the truth.

Let me reiterate that I have had other problems, and lots of them. I have done more than enough research and personal work to know my interior was loaded with alcoholic potential from a young age, and it makes sense considering so much of my experience: that a dull and fragile feeling of being over-exposed somehow, that a special effect only at the hands of a substance would fix. Alcohol, as it were, was my first love.

Also true is I exhibited what I suppose in the field of mental health diagnosis as 'borderline traits,' those familiar and ugly penchants for 'push/pull' in intimate relationships — 'I love you, but I hate you, but please come back' — crazy-making for all parties involved. That, too, was something I mentioned little, as it had no bearing on what I write here. I do believe in light of all of this was that people can recover from the way they think and the way they behave. It is a fact of my life that involved a steely determination daily to become a better man than I used to be.

Suppose there is a computer containing millions of bits of information, with a vast array of processes and functions, like something the government might use: billions of gigabytes of data circulating around, each fit to a unique purpose. If someone were to walk into the control booth with a hammer and start thrashing the control boards, the processors, the wiring harnesses, it is safe to say, this wonderful piece of technology would not function as it was meant. "How bad would the damage be? And what would change as a result?"

Well, I guess the standing damage would depend on what areas were hit the hardest. Those of us that have suffered head injury know this proposition as fact.

A woman from Denver I know reasonably well, Kathe, was telling a group of us one day about her experience having been hit so badly on the head that her motor functions and powers of speech had to be re-learned; but hanging around quietly in the forefront was a huge gap of memory loss. She recalled going to fill up her car at a gas station one day before blanking out, forgetting altogether what fueling a car *was*. She recalled being confused as to why those around her were running away in fear as she stood there with a hose of noxious liquid spraying out all over the ground.

There is another fellow, Alan, with whom I share coffee almost every week for nine months now. Alan is a brilliant college student studying for a PhD in one of the hard sciences. Somewhere back in his party years from early college, he created a disruption for which the police gave chase, not that he even did anything wrong, but he ran up a parking garage, higher and higher, laughing, genuinely enjoying the sport of being chased by the police. Finally cornered, he jumped off the fourth level, and his head hit the concrete far below, his skull shattered, and he was comatose for several months.

Alan is a brilliant man; he struggles a great deal emotionally, and on a regular occasion, a near word-salad of brilliance comes pouring out of him, in terms I think only he can truly understand. I try to reply to this with honesty. I often tell him, "I'm not sure what you are trying to say, so let me ask you: what did *you* hear yourself say?" Sometimes it seems the best way to cut to the heart of the matter.

Charles Whitman was a career military man, a loving father, a good husband when the lemon-sized tumor began growing deep within the tissue of his brain. With it came pressure on various points, and he became rabid, climbing the winding staircase to the top of a building in Austin and picking targets with the precision with a high powered rifle. One could surmise it was not really his fault. His thinking had changed, and in it, he lost control.

I cannot say I have ever lost my memory, nor had to learn the powers of speech all over again, nor had my cognition become a jumble of alphabet soup. I do not know those struggles, only my own struggles; however, in that regard, I have become an expert, if only on my own experience.

RUBBLE

Eight-to-twenty years had been an unpalatable statement. The certainty of using a bed sheet tied to the post of a jail bed loomed, which had only become a matter of timing and courage as soon as I was in booking. A friendly, older guy — clearly an ex-convict — was the only other guy sitting in the booking area that morning: a small and yellowing room encased in glass and steel doors with three barely working pay phones on the wall. He watched me come in with chemically stained hands looking odd in the white chemical suit and stated, "Wow, man. Looks like you've had an interesting morning." He asked me what I was caught with.

To the best of my knowledge, I rattled off about a dozen or so items implicating me in a case. "Yep," he said, "Sounds pretty bad. I'm not sure if there is any coming back from that." He did not need to say it out loud: I knew that. I had known that since much earlier that morning. I was just trying to… process that. It is quite a thing — no matter how bad things are going — to see the trajectory of your life change in a single moment, a verdict of living in a tomb close by.

Like a wounded animal, I hunkered down and waited to see what would happen next. And what happened next took me utterly by surprise. But it was not a good thing. In fact, it was not good at all.

No sooner had I been booked than I was asked to appear before the court, that same day, which seemed strange. Normally, there was a period where you were issued a bed in one of the lower pods if you were a low level offender, and on one of the higher floors if you had a propensity for violence or your crime entailed brandishing a weapon. You would get some jail-orange linens and at least a day or two to settle in and figure out what it was you did, and what you hoped to say that might get you out of it. I was arrested early in the morning and before the judge at two o' clock. I was brought into the misdemeanor level drug-court program, which right away I knew was a mistake. Drug court was reserved, usually, for first time offenders; it resembled something like social work with weekly appointments with the presiding judge to make sure you were doing well. Whatever they planned to charge me, it was not a joint or some loose paraphernalia. And, in this, I proved to be accurate. I stood up when called upon to do so and approached the bench as an older squat judge in a black robe thumbed through some pages, and looking puzzled, drew his own conclusion. I was dismissed right away as ineligible.

On the way back to the jail, I was separated from the rest of the small group of inmates and brought into a small, tan room with two chairs and a small table. I sat there all of twenty minutes before a clerk came in dressed in plain clothes with a stack of paperwork before him. We were both quiet while he read through some things. Finally, he shuffled the paperwork back into a neat stack, handed me a pen, and told me, "Sign right here."

"What's this?" I asked.

"Oh, this. Yes. You are being released, no bond set. Yep. You're free to go on a promise to appear."

How upward of twenty years turned into a quick signature to walk back out the door the same afternoon happened is a mystery to this day. But I did not argue, and assuming he made a mistake,

I held my breath as I was processed out, thinking at any moment they would realize their mistake and send me upstairs. But that did not happen. I strolled out the large rolling gates of the Pima County Jail, still in the paper chemical suit I was given, and started walking fast.

Initially, my friends — Tony, Chris and Terry — were happy to see me, glad I was okay. They were living in an old, pink corrugated shack off Park Avenue, reported to have been where Linda Ronstadt practiced with her backup band decades earlier. By then, it was a drug den.

Everyone already heard about everything that happened with me. I walked over to my old house later that afternoon, and the electric and water, all the utilities had been cut. The remainders of the door, with its shattered lock swayed open a sliver, had an eviction notice tacked to it. Inside, everything was destroyed, taken or scattered. What had not been taken by the police had been picked clean by whatever vultures had come though after. Just that morning, I owned a home full of belongings; by evening, I had nothing.

I stayed around Chris and Terry's a few nights, as more news poured in. The next night, another house went down, and another. The "hot-checks crowd" was rounded up and booked, and two more laboratories. This went on for a week, a giant city-wide sting operation that targeted about half of our crowd with swift precision, that same group of militarized police kicking in doors day and night all over the city. But there was one big key difference between me and the rest of this assorted and malevolent crowd. I had been the first to go down, and I had been the *only* one to get out, at least that I was aware.

It did not look good. It did not look good, at all. It smacked of having turned the others in, and that worried me, as it should have. Word was getting around quickly, from what I was told, that I was being branded as something, and it was unfavorable. And my friend Mike McDowell told me that he heard through the grapevine there were some that wished to bury me out in the desert; all that cloak and dagger stuff did not seem like such a stretch anymore. I had not done anything to anybody, but that would not matter much very soon. It did not look good at all, and I knew that. I was a dead man walking.

Somewhere in that first week or two out of jail, I called my dad collect and just like a hundred times before, had a favor to ask, but a big one this time. Through the tears, I told him the trouble I was in, painting myself somehow as the victim, and told him if there was any money left in the way of an inheritance, I needed it now for an attorney. He was devastated, but he understood the fact quite clearly. He agreed to help.

In just a matter of days, I met Alan, hired by my father to represent me. Alan was a great guy and an exceptional defense attorney. I met him downtown at his office, and I will never know, not really, what he thought about the whole situation. Initially, I was not in too terrible of shape, but as long months wore on of innate legal proceedings, this emaciated, addicted, homeless man showing up to his office, peering out the windows, who never bathed must have given him pause. If he had held judgement for my situation, he concealed it well. He usually ended up giving me ten or twenty dollars every time I saw him, probably added to a tally, I am sure, that was passed along to my family who was paying him to defend me.

It was an interesting arrangement we had, he being my sole provision of accountability in my life, waiting for my occasional phone call from a pay phone, to give an arraignment date or a pretrial conference for which I was never actually sober, or sane for that matter. One time, I had been over to his office, and really feeling desperate and hopeless. That day, he shared with me a portion of his own story about being in and out of foster care, and of being sexually abused while he was there. I think he said all of that happened in St. Louis.

I do recall, though, him relating the following: one day, after eating scraps off of the street and having woken up outdoors, he heard the tremendous sound of bells which he followed, twisting his way through the streets to get closer to the clang of these giant bells. As it were, they turned out to be church bells. When he finally found them, he stepped into that church; it was there, on that day, he was to meet who would later become his adoptive parents and put him through law school. He had a past, as well.

I do not remember exactly at what point I abandoned my legal proceedings and any hope of completing them, only that I had, deciding — instead — to become an absconder, which in court terms was a 'failure to appear.' I may have already been probated; there is something, after all, to be said of the power of a good attorney, and — I dare say — white privilege. All I remember is as soon as a private attorney took over my case, the possible outcome changed, and radically so. What seemed to be a lengthily sentence became a simple one-to-four-year prison term with the possibility of probation. Even after hearing that, having had a ray of hope open up in what felt like a death sentence, I knew from past experience what they would ask of me was an impossibility; I was broken and mangled, my thoughts a jumbled mess of bad wiring; even basic employment felt far beyond my reach. So, I never went back; I decided to rot instead.

I became more brazen in every action I took, walking out of convenience stores with an armful of stolen items hoping to be shot in the back. A great vacuum inside me swallowed as much poison as was available in disporting fashion, any lingering concern of my ability to handle it, pushed aside easily. On one occasion, I closed my eyes and stepped off a curb. I heard a shout as a car swerved to avoid me and motors past.

I have heard many in recovery in some form or fashion say they knew they were going to die, chalking that up to what I suppose might be a frightful intellectual process. I thought that before, sure. But something happened in that last year, difficult to explain, but with a soundness and absolution to it, unlike anything I had known prior. What I began to experience was not a thought of dying, but a certainty and feeling that it was already happening. I would sometimes sit on a park bench and sadly muse at what had become of me and the ending at hand, and feel a quiet regret. There was a little joy found, also, in the thought that I was a happy kid; there were some good times, some good things to look back. I no longer feared it. I resolved myself totally over to it, welcomed the curtain to fall and pull me out of this barren desert of consequence.

****

I am twenty-nine now. I know this only because my mother told me so. We arrange for a meetup point near an arroyo where I sleep in the sand. She brings me a sleeping bag with a big, pink bow on it and tells me that it is "going to be a cold winter." Facing the brunt of the summer before had been no easy task either.

I roam the streets, unintelligible chatter pouring from my mouth. I lash out at imaginary foes, or mumble along, sometimes asking passersby for money. I don't know, but it feels like I broke my left foot which is, now, wrapped in duct tape. I stop occasionally, picking up a piece of trash on the ground and turn it over it my hands. My sunken eyes can't stand the light anymore, and the s un blisters and suffocates me. I am a ghost in what feels like an endless urban Sahara.

****

Generally, I steered wide of the other homeless many of whom settled in quiet, if not happy, routines. Some learned to expect a check a certain time of the month, others built an organized camp with everything they needed at hand: a mattress, sometimes a small shelf for books; some kept ice in a thermos nearby, or a bucket and soap for washing clothes. But I was not like them, did not wish to be. I walked; sometimes I slept; and I hid. And yet, a deep unrest would never quite allow me to be still.

And so I walked, to nowhere in particular before turning around and walking back, often upward of twenty miles a day I would guess, which is a nomadic and burdensome plight only those who have lived it might truly understand. As I came to find out, in soaked and sour clothes, my presence was unwanted at every turn, with posted placards and signs of every type telling me so: 'No loitering. No Panhandling. No Sleeping. No Sitting.' When the signs went unheeded, there was always some store manager or park employee urging me to get up and go, go be somewhere else. And I always did: the walking dead searching for rest.

There is a point in the unravelling of a life where the basic social functions of a person deteriorate altogether, where the very basis of living becomes savage, animal-like. Concerns of brushed teeth, of looking well, of trying to blend into the room or of making a good impression, become lost altogether. Eating and sleeping and searching for comfort take over, a living pyramid of basic needs as it were. In that state, all things become possibilities, simply as a matter of survival. One of my proclivities on those long walks had been to check every car handle along the way, searching for unlocked doors. Ashtray change, mostly, is what I looked for, just enough to get through a day, which often involved up to forty cars in a long piece of mileage walked. On a couple of occasions, I slipped out of the driver's seat and turned unwittingly to the owner of the car, angry and red-faced, one time getting pummeled before even getting out of the front seat; but usually, the results of my efforts went a bit better. The smallest inkling of conscience, even then, was prone to kick in. Every time I saw children's toys on the floor of the car, or a child seat in the back, my eyes would get wet against my own will, and a deep well of humanity would raise up, causing me to walk away no matter how bad I hurt; the same could be said of finding a coin marking a length of recovery time. Like kryptonite, these drove me off, a vampire cast back out into the street searching for something else.

On a handful of occasions, rummaging through a vehicle, I would find a spare car key hidden in the ashtray. The first time, I took a long pause. Not so long earlier, the idea of stealing a car would have been unfathomable. But with aching legs and needing respite, the decision was made seemingly for me: an easier way to travel and someplace to rest my legs for a while as I drove. When paranoia would set in in a week's time or so, not wanting to be pulled over — to be *caught* — I would sell the car for twenty dollars, usually to someone who spoke very little English.

I recall one day driving about, sleepless, crazy. I had not slept in a couple of days and ended up behind a gas station off of

Speedway Boulevard. Dawn was creeping up, and I passed out behind the wheel, slumped over, only to re-emerge when the sun was high. I remember rubbing the sleep from my eyes with balled fists and looking down at what appeared to be a small snack tray, packaged with crackers and a small tub of cheese in a small plastic container, sitting in my lap. Attached to it was a sticky note that read, "I'll be praying for you. Good luck." My window had been rolled down over night, and the slightest of gestures from someone who operated from a much higher plane of morality reached into my life, leaving a gift. I recall that well, a sliver of light in pure darkness.

Whatever danger I faced with my prior associates became a dark tide that stole me out to sea almost daily. I always looked over my shoulder and around corners. I relocated, largely, to a neighborhood known as 'Savaco,' which meant armpit in Spanish. I knew nobody there, and almost no one spoke English. I felt safe, tucked away and out of sight. I had one friend, a dope dealer by the name of Max who often invited me in for menudo or some other breakfast his madre cooked for him, and those were lucky days indeed. Most mornings proved to be far glummer. There was an old church with its faded paint façade across the front proclaiming 'Victory' in cursive letters, and sometimes, old loaves of bread would be outback. I was never sure if they were left over from some sort of pantry aid program, but I would grab some slices from a torn open bag and head over to a small fast food joint on west St. Mary's. There, I would go to the condiment counter during breakfast and take a handful of jelly packets or ketchup packets, and that was usually my only meal of the day. I had no interest in soup lines or homeless shelters because I had no interest in other people. Much like an animal that has been afflicted with grave illness, I preferred solitude, much like they choose a shrub under which to die, peaceful and alone.

Even during my troubles legally, my mind still raced with thoughts of chemical compounds, fragments of recipes and periodic tables. Somewhere back then, I went for a walk stopping in late night at a grocer and sliding up the home aisle, opening a small, plastic container full of red devil lye, pouring just a bit into an old, used sandwich baggy I snuck in in my pocket. If I had been seen at all, I was never confronted. I slipped out of the store and walked through the quiet weirdness of that night, walking several miles. I felt something like a sunburn happening beneath my jeans, a glowing spot on my upper thigh, which I ignored altogether. When I arrived at my hovel — I made my own — I pulled out the bag half-full of lye, just then noticing the small hole in the corner. Pulling down my jeans, there was a steaming black, well, hole on my leg, burned down into the muscle. The next day it looked like someone glued a large slice of jerky to my leg with a thick scab of burnt flesh stuck to it. I showed it to my mother the next time I saw her, who started to cry.

There were places, small enclaves, where a measure of safety would steal over me. I dragged some type of store awning into a dry creek-bed setting up a fire near it, or putting together a small place behind a wall near a large building downtown, a blanket laid out in the leaves and a stack of books and old shirts nearby, trying to make something, anything, feel like a home. There were a few of us for a time, other younger people whom called themselves "travelers" who had cut a hole in a fence of a giant yard full of old, retired ambulances. The disemboweled ambulances served us for a time; we would use rocks to break the windows out, and lay down in the gurney ports to sleep. Like the others, it was short lived, knowing those were always temporary, one day — soon enough — to find things tossed or wrecked, urging all to pick up and get to somewhere else, on a long path, to nowhere.

And whilst most days had the same monotone to them, as interesting as breaking rocks in a field, other days took on the sentiment of passerby, either in the way of undeserved kindness or intolerable cruelty. I had been asleep on the side of a small Carneceria, a meat market, on the west side one day, when abruptly, I was woken. A tall and very business dressed white woman was kneeling down, hovering over me. My eyes fluttered open. She had a concerned look, a stricken face. "You... you're not okay. Here," she said, rummaging through her purse and fishing out a ten-dollar bill. "Here. Take this. Put this deep in your pocket, don't let anyone take it from you," she said, thrusting the bill my way. "I wish... I wish there was..." she started trailing off. She stood up and walked around the corner to wherever she was headed.

On another day, I built a little fort, complete with a small fire pit, a pot and a pan, a small but paltry stack of the only things I had left: an old Sony Walkman, a baseball hat, some sunglasses. Everything was strewn out on a disaster blanket behind a wall of a historic site downtown; I had been there for just a day or two. It was early that morning, after daylight had barely broken. I heard footsteps in the dirt as someone approached. In a grey tidy-looking shirt, and black slacks stood a rented security guard. He was looming over me, grinning. I sat up a little bit, got on my knees as I went to stand, feeling a confrontation at hand.

"Hey you." He said, leering, chewing a toothpick in his wide and toothy grin. "Do you know what, pal?" he said, again, with that broad grin. "I had to take a *shit* the other day, a really *big one*," he continued, chuckling. "So, I came back here to take it. I took it *right there*." He told me while pointing at my blanket splayed across the ground. "Yeah, that's right," he added, before continuing. "Don't look so confused. I took a shit right there. Right there where you sleep. You are pretty much sleeping in my *shit*."

With one hand, he rubbed his fat belly, hoisting his trousers up; with the other hand, he twirled a toothpick in his mouth. "Ha," he said, laughing a bit. In that moment, I felt a white, hot something, a feeling I had never known. I noticed his belt with a radio but devoid of any real protection, and he stood there leering, marveling in his seeming victory while I sat quiet. My eyes went to the river rock holding down the corner of my blanket, smooth to the touch, maybe five or six pounds. My hand crept toward it, him being none the wiser. I pictured that rock in my hand, cracking open his head like a large melon. Three maybe four good hits before his pinkish brain matter would spill out, and I could drag him into the bushes with me, into my bed, into the growth of the surrounding hedge, and knew how easy it would be. As I reached for the rock, he did an about face, trailing off with, "I don't want to see you back here again," whistling as he strolled around the corner. My teeth were clenched, fighting back murder in my throat, in my chest, a steaming vapor in my head. Then, he was gone.

Illness, in its progression, always takes on different forms. Just months prior, in the safety of my home, my tolerance for substances of various kinds was sky high. I would literally do hundreds of dollars' worth of substances in two-day's time, sometimes not having felt much of anything. By the nature of how I lived, an endless supply was always around. But homelessness had been a bleak existence, little money and very few ways of getting anything had reduced a large habit to a much smaller one; the progression, however, was the lengths I would go through to get it.

I had been walking in a rainstorm one day, with a tiny cellophane of tar heroin tucked securely away in my sock. I walked into a fast food joint; this was where all the homeless in that part of city went to get high, many of whom died in some unfortunate restaurant's bathroom. Soaking wet, I locked myself in the restroom before management could object. I was crushed to pull up my pant leg to see what had been tidy cellophane had ruptured, and the tar become a brown spot on an old, dirty sock I had been wearing for weeks. Undeterred, I tried my best to wring out that sock into a spoon on the countertop. All that mattered was "medicine."

****

Three hundred sixty days.

When some sense of cognition came to me a month or so later, I looked at a calendar to see just how long I had been displaced; God knows it felt like forever. It is a number, today, I am fond. Three hundred sixty days emaciated: of walking forever, of building small fires behind factories, of sleeping on top of a parking garage, of being both a spectacle and invisible all at the same time, of being reduced to savagery and unparalleled craving. The fruition of the damage done decades before, finally, overtaking me; the torment of things in my mind I had long pictured, finally, materializing as reality.

BROKEN HEARTS

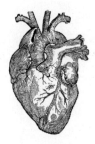

I suppose there comes a point in the lives of some of us, where the only thing remaining that seems real is our own pain. The self-involvement of one's own hell becomes exclusionary to all other things, and those on the sidelines merely become an afterthought, their tears a faraway rainstorm in a distant land.

I can tell you about that.

I was, after a time, a cancerous and painful tumor in my family; my dad would describe me, years later, as "the one dark cloud in a bright sky," which he added, "never went away." My own suffering became unfathomable and intolerable; in a very peculiar way, for someone so adverse to pain, I seemed to both attract and create a great deal of it. But for those who stood on the sidelines, spectators of a loved one being mauled to death, content to extinguish his own life, that same pain seemed to have been transferred over. What I know today and have painstakingly listened to, led me to the conclusion that during those ugly and tragic years — at the very least — I created my own medicine for a time that seemed to work. My family was aptly *sober,* and coherent through all of it. They could not numb it out or push it somewhere else.

When I was concussed the first time, I share that my mother played both tennis and golf. She took up black and white photography, trying to pull from her inner soul both meaning and artwork. She, on occasion, would host a neighborhood party for women who sold cosmetics and would come over and have some type of spa day. Years later, when I was thirty, my mom took sleeping pills and went to bed at 7:30 at night, reclusive and tucked away in a quiet life of mystery novels, and a job that kept her content by day. Dreams of the past had turned out to be just that, dreams; those eventually took a dark turn when the youngest in the family, her son, would come apart and be all but obliterated by the streets. However mangled I became — in both thought and behavior — it seemed like it aged my own mother fifty years, and I would be remiss not to mention this.

Three years ago, maybe a month or so before I moved to Dallas, my mother and I went out to dinner at a Mexican restaurant. We mused over many things, as I have made it a point to keep things light and airy with my folks, as much as I can; though sometimes, we will take a brief trip through the past together, as we did on that evening.

"After the incident," she said, pausing. "You know… you remember which one. I went to mass that morning and I went twenty minutes early. So, I could be alone. I remember asking God that morning, if he could kill you, if he could just… *take you.* I knew I couldn't help anymore, and I knew I couldn't try. So, I gave you, to him," she said, her eyes tearing up.

I felt that.

I think, looking back, I would recover long before that of my mother, who had a tough life growing up, that in many ways only got harder as the years went on.

My sister was more cynical and hardened by my life, where — to her — I became something like competition for our parent's affection. No matter how high she soared academically, I was always there to overshadow her success with a car accident, jail stays, a dark distraction from what ought to have been well earned praise. My sister learned soon on to give me little. Though, there was a time when she gave some reprieve by letting me sleep in her car for a period of a month or so. I would slink through the shadows and curl up in a ball on the back seat, always hoping for a half-extinguished cigarette butt in her car ashtray to light up in the dark, before putting myself to sleep.

Years later, I approached her with a letter I wrote, recognizing in a very real way how somewhere years earlier, I shredded her photo album and stole a tiny piece of her life in that sense. I, also, stole a little money and a bottle of vodka somewhere along the way. I explained these things, expressing regret.

"Let me stop you right there!" She said curtly. *"You don't have a fucking clue what you've done to this family!"*

I listened as she talked. I listened as she told me about going to work one day at a high school where she normally did not teach but had been called in as a substitute. She told me she, on that day, stopped at a convenience store near the university football stadium to refill her coffee thermos. She got out of her car to see her brother, me, pale and unconscious on the sidewalk with a weak pulse and shallow breathing. She recalled she "did not know what to do." In a deep and unsettled confusion, she decided she would soon be late, and stepped over me like a piece of garbage on the street; she went to teach eight periods of class that day, fighting back tears the entire time.

When she told me that, I felt every word of it.

It is for her sake, for all of their sakes, that I write this as recognition of their days spent in worry, trying to control their emotions and push through an embattled life, caring for a fallen son and brother who — in the end — had been buried mentally by them out of sheer necessity.

It took years and thousands of dollars coupled with a great deal of humility to go back through my past, righting every wrong, facing down every insult and injury I could see that I caused, and set those matters right, to take my place as a brother and a son. Repeatedly for upward of a decade, I traced the routes back through early childhood, righting every wrong ever done, paying every debt ever owed. Often, confessing for actions to whom the recipient was none the wiser. All but one, if memory serves, went well. More than anything else, including some modalities written about later, it may have been what saved me.

IN THE FLESH

On November 21st — sixteen years ago as of this writing — I went
into a blackout induced by taking a handful of medication that was
not prescribed to me, and of which the usage I cannot be sure. I
was bewildered and heavily disorientated when I re-emerged to
something like a conscious state, and because the sky was bathed
in pinks and yellows, I remember I was not sure if the sun was
rising or setting. As it turned out, I lost a good number of hours in
that blackout with little-to-no inclination that the most remarkable
event that was about to occur, and the terrific beating that would
set a chain of events in motion.

    Turns out, it was around noon, standing at the corner of
Sixth Street and Sixth Avenue in Tucson, which housed an auto
body shop, a screen printing shop and a handful of houses, one
of which belonged to a guy named Derek who made both a habit
and a lifestyle of filling his yard with reclaimed junk of every type,
shape and purpose: children's bikes, broken tables, wooden desks,
Xerox machine parts, all strewn around a rock garden with pieces
of colored, broken glass carefully outlining it. It was the doings

and artwork one might associate with active schizophrenia. Derek was a quiet, gentle soul who harbored several street types, extra convicts and anyone else whom he found interesting.

I stayed there for a bit and had an "on-again/off-again" relationship with him. One time, I feigned an attack with a fire axe with someone in his living room; I do not recall any intention to chop into the guy — and for the life of me, I cannot remember what started that off — but another hanger-on in that group tackled me, with my axe, into a struggling heap on the ground, and I was invited to leave. It was the typical nonsensical goings-on of those who lived deviant lifestyles, and the ensuing drama that was created.

On this day, I dropped by Derek's for a moment when someone who had been staying there who simply went by "Bull" — with his squat muscular frame, arms full of prison tattoos and handlebar mustache — approached me at the gate and got into my face about something he thought I stole or something he thought I did. Wanting nothing to do with Bull, I began to backpedal verbally, but before I could lay out whatever my alibi was to escape, I had been sucker punched cleanly in the mouth, knocking me off my feet and into the dirt. I stood up surprised, rubbing my jaw. "Fuck man. You didn't have to do that."

Mercifully, Bull did not come at me further, verbally or otherwise. Still holding my face, I stumbled down Sixth Avenue headed south beneath the bridge with its uric odor and toward downtown. I had a friend, a guy I knew from high school named Andy. Andy worked for a street clinic, social work type of agency, which dealt with harm reduction for the homeless, everything from food boxes to clean syringes to helping set up dental appointments for folks that had no insurance or means to get any.

****

I have not slept — not really — in five days. My kick was a writhing and unsettling roller coaster of sickened flesh, vacillating between awful and something much worse. The medication, Librium, helps some and I am grateful for it. A smell and taste of sulfur — which is something new — fills my mouth for days. On day five, sleep overtakes me.

I am dreaming now. I am in a schoolyard. The air seems bright and clear. It is the air I knew on the beach as a child, air filled with the wonder and color of spring. I see a gymnasium, and without thought, I climb it. I climb and I climb, reaching for new bars that appear out of thin air, and I step on rungs below as the others fall away. It is a transient and shifting structure, dissipating as I climb, higher, then even higher. I am aware, somehow, this dream is like none other before. I realize — soundly — I am terrified of heights, terrified to fall; I always have been, and I have never not been. Except, this time, I am not. Clouds part; things open up. A tapestry with the distant glow of milky, white stars coats the sky, and I see the world here, fearless and open. A landscape full of wonder. A bright feeling shoots through me, and I laugh. Laughing in the clouds...............

I wake up. And I know, sure as I have ever known anything ever before,
I am different.

****

Merely two weeks sober, I sat in a lecture provided by a counselor named Les, somewhere in those early weeks of sobriety with twenty or so other charges who sat through educational groups, either itching from the inside out to get out of this place to get another drink somehow, or trying to give their derided attention to Les who was explaining the ill after effects of prolonged bouts of drinking. Les had been grooming himself for expanding his roles and duties, and as such, had taken up setting up a video camera to record his lectures, grading them on content and presentation. He told all of us this, of course, upon starting the lecture, and told us that he was really working on trying to cut out his apt penchant for curse words from his verbose but otherwise enjoyable group sessions. In this, he failed miserably: I counted three times he said 'pack of assholes' and twice he said "it's a bunch of bullshit." It let me know we all had room for improvement.

That morning though, we were watching a slide presentation on something referred to as 'PAWS,' or post-acute withdrawal symptoms, to which we might all reasonably stand to be affected, especially those of us — like myself — who had burned the candle bright at both ends for quite some time. Symptoms might include short attention span, short memory, and a host of other nefarious repercussions of having drank or used drugs for far too long. We sat on folding metal chairs, counting down the clock, fading in and out of the lecture, as those of us who smoked kept careful track of the timing of our next cigarette.

The lecture had me pegged already at that point: I was liable to lose my house key upward of ten times a day, and each time was sneakily suspicious that someone stolen it, or maybe was attempting to get over on me somehow. Trips to the grocery store, I would twirl my keys around on my finger, contemplating basic life choices such as cheerios or frosted flakes, and absently set them down atop the boxes of the aisle before wandering off with zero recollection of where I had just been, or the fact that I left my keys there. It was as near to temporary amnesia as one could imagine, but my responsibilities were few, and my only job, at that point, was simply to survive myself on a day-to-day basis. And so it was, wallets, sunglasses, keys, pencils, pens, notebooks, belts, really anything smaller than say a clock radio, were scattered about on a daily basis, which turned into an agitated treasure hunt.

I, also, experienced a thought-life that seemed blasted into a thousand fragments, like a brick hitting a windowpane. Thoughts would come and not complete themselves; I would think of something important to say, and it would turn to vapor after vocalizing maybe half of it. My thoughts were a gradient of sliced Swiss, elusive and hard to capture.

I would like to tell you the timeline I was given in that lecture held true for me, but nothing could be further from the truth. I *did* exemplify everything the counselor, Les, talked about, but in my case, the duration of it seemed to stretch on and on like a desert.

I became known around that treatment campus, and later in my first couple of places of employment, as having a quirky personality wherein most of the sentences I started would simply remain unfinished. It was commonplace for me to walk up and say, "You know, I've been thinking...we really ought to try, I mean, really try..." before blinking and glazing over and wandering off to whatever duty had me previously engaged. My good friends called it "Pulling a 'Jeff Gould'," and it was a move I pulled often. Walking out of conversations before any conclusion had been reached became my style, though not on purpose.

Around this time, I ran into an old friend — a tattoo artist named Mike — in the grocery store. Having been sober but a few months, I remember standing in the milk and dairy aisle before receiving a tap on the shoulder, "Jeff?" I turned around and greeted my old friend, "Oh, hey Mike. Good to see you."

He had what looked to be a sense of utter disbelief, a puzzled but pleased look from someone who, on multiple occasions, tried to hold me accountable to doing the right things as I slid down the drain and into homelessness. It was, for the record, neither the first nor the last time I received that look, the look of someone who has literally seen a dead man walking and the breath of life itself show up in instead. The lights were coming back on for me; I felt vitally healthy, and I looked better than I ever had in my life.

I was always rail-thin, but in those final days of being cast out to the streets, mainly by personal choice, my ordinarily thin frame become near skeletal. The last time I was to step upon a scale before sobering up it would register one hundred twenty pounds. My mom, somewhere near the end of that desperate period of my life, accused me of flat-out trying to starve myself to death, which was not true as far as motives went, but I succumbed to this phenomenon of immense craving in which food became an afterthought and held no priority whatsoever.

It was good to see Mike; we gave each other a pretty big hug, and he, again, just looked at me in wonder and said, "I don't know what you are doing man, but whatever it is, promise me you'll keep doing it." And that was a promise I intended to keep.

Having said that, the first year or two of stepping into a new basis of life had twists and turns and, at times, were laden with difficulty that even now, I wonder how I ever pushed through them. Waves of darkness would come and go, and sleep was something that had not come easily, and even today, still does not.

That place, the place I was staying, was a state-sponsored twenty-eight day spin-dry place. It was actually about one hundred eighty units of what used to be some run-down apartments, with a handful of counselors and case managers who lived there in the fairly crime-filled neighborhood where Stone Avenue and Glenn Street intersected. I always knew that corner as it had a giant Paul Bunyan statue that was there since I was a kid.

Something that struck me as peculiar almost immediately was my inability to sleep. That was the first time in years I had a soft, comfortable mattress, clean linens, soft pillows, yet for days, I laid there, twisting and turning, listening to the soft hush of my roommate breathing unable to drift off in the comfort of that nice bed. I would get up and walk about for a while, left with my own thoughts in the early morning hours. In a downstairs unit, there was a rather lumpy and spring-loaded couch fit for a landfill. It had a few clothed edges from a well-worn and fractured chassis beneath its cushions. I think it might have been the third or fourth night I poured myself onto it, and opened the window to the cold, November desert air. From the street below, sound of police sirens, tires screeching, and the distant blur of sounds from Tommy's Lounge up the street filled my senses and lulled me into deep and dreamless sleep.

Of course, when my twenty-eight-day tenure was up, I had nowhere to go, no wife to go back to, no relatives to take me in, no money to go and apply for housing. My counselor enrolled me to stay longer, for which I was grateful; I did not know then, but longer was to turn into an eleven month stay, with a short departure of having spent forty-two days in jail, staring down my past, when I turned myself over to the authorities for having been a fugitive during the past year: a no-show for a previously set court date from the laboratory charges I picked up.

I was starting to feel the benefits of having developed a spiritual practice, as well as having ate and slept like a normal person for the first time in years. I tried not to think about court; well, really, I tried not to think about going back to jail sitting atop a hot bunk with foul smelling odors emanating from whomever

I might be stuck with, staring out that bulletproof two-inch wide windowpane, watching the world breeze by.

When I decided, some months later, that my only option was to turn myself over and let whatever was going to happen, happen, I did not fight it. My friend, Mike, helped me get in contact with the attorney who would have represented me before had I not absconded. That was on a Tuesday; and on Wednesday morning, I found myself standing near the bright sixteen-foot-tall fence lined with razor wire, ringing a buzzer, in effect, to be let it. I was gently nudged to turn toward the fence, when a friendly enough officer told me, "You have the right to remain silent. Anything you say can and will be used against you..." before being led inside.

I spent — up to that point in my life — almost ten months in jail, in various lengths and terms, which for me, simply put, never got any easier. It always proved to be a soul-crushing experience that seemed to arouse a loneliness and longing for family that, admittedly, I never really felt when I was outside its walls. Trying to fit in with a crowd of others and their derelictions, or avoid falling prey to some game, the likes of which was constructed by sociopaths, made for unhappy work. I learned, of course, years before from a fellow inmate: don't gamble; stay to yourself; don't disrespect anybody; stick to two or three people you get along with, and read as much as possible.

Which is not to say, at some point in an earlier stay, there were not comical episodes which I was keen on being involved. The main jail, the big tower, had this massive, powerful plumbing system used for its five hundred plus toilets; to flush one felt like kick starting a jet engine, and you could feel the suction coming off it. One time, my cellmate wanted to see how many bedsheets he could flush down a toilet without clogging it; the answer turned out to be three, with a bonus of a very puzzled corrections officer who could have sworn he gave us fresh sheets the afternoon before.

This stay though, what would turn out to be forty-two days, would be unlike any others. My attorney had — in good faith — convinced the judge that I was a non-flight risk, even though my history indicated otherwise; turning myself in did prove to have merit. I was actually furloughed pending my court proceedings, which meant that Monday through Friday, I would be let out to go wash dishes for the French restaurant where I started working three months prior.

After about a week, I was transferred over to what they call the Mission: a giant monolith of a holding which had four separate, giant, concrete rooms full of bunks; two were for the trustees who held jobs within the jail, and the other two were for those of us privileged to have work release.

I remember being transported over there with a few other guys in a van holding a plastic cup which contained a few toiletries and my street clothes, neatly folded in a pile, and a couple of extra pairs of jail-issued orange suits. There was a guard — a tall, muscular black guy — who seemed to know me from years prior as my mom had been his nurse practitioner who helped keep his diabetes under control. I saw him on a number of occasions over the years, always locked up, and he always gave me a pretty stern lecture on not being such a shithead and overwhelming disappointment to my parents.

"Your mom is good people," he told me once. "You need to knock it the fuck off with whatever it is you are up to." Whether it actually was or not, I told myself that his sentiments came from a place of concern, and I knew if nothing else, he respected my mom and I could appreciate that. This time though, he said something else: "Dude. What are you doing here? You don't...*look* like you belong here, at all."

I think I caught him off guard probably. I had an extra fifty pounds on me; my hair was combed; my eyes were bright, and I had a stack of books under my arm that I checked out from the Chaplains cart. I was quick to tell him, "I am doing great, and I've never felt better. I'm just here, cleaning up some old messes," and added it was good to see him, too.

I shared a bunk with a Polynesian guy, very small in stature, who mostly looked like a sixth grader with a moustache. Apparently, he had been in a blackout and fired a few shots from a shotgun through the ceiling, and that was pretty much what brought him to being there; he seemed receptive, so I told him what I knew about being sober, which I remember served him very well. He had been sober a few years the last time we spoke.

Through what might only be described as a legal miracle of sorts, I was released on day forty-two. I was given a probation term of four years to complete, and this was very much against the prosecutors recommendation and liking. It was on that day I was asked to approach the bench with the judge, with his leathery complexion and silver hair combed back over his ears, looking intently down a court docket reading the charges. He said something like, "Mr. Gould, would you mind telling me what 'attempt to possess equipment used to manufacture a dangerous drug' means? I mean, what is it?"

I think the courts effort to strike a plea deal had, in fact, muddied the waters as to what actually occurred, and what I had actually done. I do not quite remember but saying something like this in response: "Your honor, whatever it says I did, I did do. That, and more. I am just here because I have been taught to be accountable for my actions, and whatever you think best suits me in terms of consequence, I am at peace with."

I do not know if I was *at peace* with it, but I do remember trying to be. He, then, told me, "This is the last chance you are ever going to get. Don't run again." The prosecutions desk started to object and interject, before he shut them down, and continued with the terms I was to meet. And just like that, I was free.

I pin-balled around a bit, direction-less, in those first couple of years of convalescing. I worked at the French place until I was promoted to the salad station, where the familiar and unflinching pile of dishes I battled every day took on the form of tickets that demanded higher thinking: extra tomato, no onion, or extra onion, no tomato and substitute Greek dressing for champagne vinaigrette. The details made me want to break things, and the more mistakes I made, the more overwhelmed I felt. Likewise, the more overwhelmed I became, I created a landscape of new mistakes. It was a salad-based disaster on all fronts.

My next temporary gig was putting together caterings for the community college. I learned about table skirts and chaffing pans; I learned to stand with my hands folded, and wear white gloves, standing by as if a butler, ready to serve. The insult was the clip-on bow tie though, which to this day I have never resolved myself to wearing. It was short-lived, however. I was hired pending a background investigation, and when that part of the process was complete, I was told I could not be trusted to drive their fan to do the caterings I was hired to do. I was not crazy about the job, so it was an easy let down.

Life back then had a funny synchronicity to it: every time something needed to happen, it did. I think, if memory serves, the same day I had been let off the hook for the catering, my good friend in early recovery, Tom, called me, asking if I wanted to work in pest control. That was the beginning of what would be the next year of my life, driving a tanker full of termiticide with heavy boxes of tools lining it and a giant drill called a roto-hammer for pounding through the concrete slabs of people's homes to try to spray the termites presumably beneath.

Our team was an array of maladapted but otherwise hard workers. My understanding of the guy I replaced was that he actually had been a pretty good worker who, some suspected, smoked way too much pot. In the last couple weeks of his employment, he drilled a hole through an exterior wall and stuck his wand through it, dousing about a hundred thousand dollars' worth of paintings on the other side. One could only imagine what his thinking had been.

I had not been worthy of much trust for the past decade. Therefore, I took pride in my big termite truck, and the fact alone that I was actually allowed to take it home at night meant something to me. But that said, the hours were often long, driving around ten hours by myself in the hot sun, only pairing up with other employees on much bigger jobs.

My initial partner, Jeff, was a wonderful family man who — I learned in my teachings about alcoholism — was a 'periodic.' He drank, or rather, went out drinking to the adult nightclub by the airport with the wonderfully appropriate name of Turbulence maybe three or four times a year; each time, it was a disaster of great magnitude that would leave his last debauch paling in comparison, prompting his wife to pack up their newly born son and head to her mother's house, threatening divorce. Jeff would always come limping back after his three- or four-day benders, put on some sort of work probationary status until things cooled off. On one occasion, we received a call from the office that our pest control truck had been driving down an alley going almost a hundred miles an hour early in the wee hours of the morning, which did not play out well.

Trent was the other guy I was apt to be paired with, and who himself had a history of failings and challenges both. Trent was really an oversized seven-year-old whose driver's license stated he was nearing the age of fifty, but it was hard to tell with him. I do remember one time, we had been driving around on the northwest side of town, and he asked me, "Do you want to see where I live?" I knew from some previous talking's with him he was at his mom's, but on that day, we had just a few accounts, so I told him, "Sure. Let's go."

He got excited and clapped his big, meaty hands together three times, excited as a person could be to take me to his house. We walked in, and of course, I met his mother who looked as dated as the house itself: that weird popcorn stuff decorating the low hanging ceilings, shag carpet, and a certain smell I have always associated with mothballs. "Want to see my room?" Trent asked, and again, I agreed.

We went to the end of the hall, and I took pause when I saw that Trent's room — quite literally — had not changed much since he was a kid. He slept on a single boy's bed with Denver Broncos sheets, next to it a Denver Broncos lamp in the shape of a football helmet. There might have been a poster of the Hulk on the wall, and all I could manage was, "This is really great. You are...really lucky." Be that as it may, Trent was always kind of a joyful guy to be around, and he had a story that was — as I like to say — "one for the books."

Somewhere back when, in his own misadventures of drug or alcohol fueled mayhem, he did something which had the local PD issue a warrant for his arrest; from the way he told it, he had been participating in a children's school play when the warrant was served, twirling around in tights dressed as a leafy plant, when he was blindsided and tackled from a group of police who identified him from backstage.

I will never truly know if he was telling the truth, but the picture in my head of this overweight but jubilant man being taken down in the middle of a school play always appealed to my somewhat dark sense of humor.

At around the eleven-month mark, the long hot days and flying solo all the time proved to be, in the end, not for me. I grew up somewhat, but the lesson of giving a two-week notice in good standing had not yet set in; so it turned out, the day that I turned my keys in — again, in that natural way of perfect timing — was the same day that the phone rang, again, for work. Only this time, it was driving a van for county mental health.

Those first years of sobriety, I was still pretty savage, like a rhesus monkey with social consciousness, or a really centered and grounded ten-year-old. Often, the front of my shirt was covered in cigarette ash or mustard stains, and I was prone to fits and outbursts of anger at the slightest provocation that, say, a fax machine was going to start in on me, giving me a hard time by not doing whatever it was I expected it to do. My memory was frightfully bad in almost every area and remains so today; the shorter the term, the worse it gets. If you were to loan me a pencil in the last three minutes and suddenly make an inquiry into its whereabouts, with a gun to my head, I could not give you a straight answer.

The job at the county detox was a perfect fit only in the sense that it had little-to-no responsibility, save for the transportation to other hospitals or taking people home daily. It gave me a great deal of time dealing with people exactly like myself, even though I was only removed from the same circumstance by a good handful of months. Whatever dereliction was going on in Tucson that I had not met before, I began to know on a first name basis.

In the summers, everything walking in the door was certainly worse for wear, being in one hundred fourteen degrees with no mindfulness to the basic necessities, like drinking water, will tear up a human being. One younger guy, a cocaine addict, had been walking barefoot on the sidewalk for a couple of days, and his feet were covered in second degree burns. Still another was a short and gangly type with protruding eyes sunk in the back of his head showing the peculiar angles of his skull beneath. He always had this furry Kangal hat pulled down over his head, but in his triage on the day he arrived, we noticed he kept slipping his hand up under it and fidgeting around up there.

This, of course, drew the triage nurse's curiosity, and she asked him to take off his hat, which he was highly averse to doing. He sat on the plastic chair, pulling it down even further, suddenly looking a bit frightened. "Sir, again, I'm going to have to ask you to take off your hat."

When he finally complied, it appeared that — like a great number of the meth patients we would see — he had been what we called a "picker:" someone who would spend hours picking away at imaginary mites under their skin, only in his case, there was a small orb of bone on the top of his head where he had picked away for weeks until a small circular area of white skull-bone was exposed. I never would have imagined, prior to that, that such things were possible.

We had one guy, older type, nice enough, who was of the chronic alcoholic variety, a street person, the very epitome of 'hobo' with overalls, a red bandana around his neck, long, grey beard. He had the soul of a poet and indicated in our conversations that he felt the measure of a man was how much grocery store brand vodka one could drink while remaining standing. His name was Lance, which I usually pictured as being a metrosexual finance type; thus, it did not fit him, but I would always make time to talk with him when he was on the ward, which was — like clockwork — about every six weeks, and the gradual slope from life to death hung around him like an overcoat.

The last time I saw him, Lance had come onto the unit, his head now shaved with metal staples holding his skull back together, upward of perhaps fifty of them though I did not count. He had an alter ego in there somewhere who, in the midst of his blackouts, liked to challenge others who would often oblige him. Hence, every once in a while, he would lose a few days, wake up having nearly been murdered, not knowing how or whom he provoked, only that he had clearly done so. Lance quit coming around after a while, and I assumed and hoped, he found some peace.

I was making eight and a quarter an hour, which was a marked improvement from the five fifty I used to from some of the kitchen jobs I held years before. It paid the meager sliver of rent, provided a few groceries, and a few tanks of gas. Back then, I had little more than a TV on a milk crate that I rummaged from behind a grocery store, a mattress on the floor, a couple of pots and pans and a big, clunky PC computer. But, to me, it felt like a castle; and every night I walked into the safety and inclusion of it; waking up there always felt a bit like heaven. It was a long-sought piece of stability after years of disarray.

I got offered a job which, at first, appeared to be a better one and paid seventy-five cents more an hour than what I previously earned, so I jumped at the chance: working on a twelve-bed program for combat veterans from mainly our first go-around in the gulf. Many had the all-too-familiar signs of emotional distress and combat fatigue, though most of them were just good, old-fashioned alcoholics.

I would be there five days a week helping manage a bright variety of pills of every type: water pills, nitro for heart conditions, anti-depressants, acid reflux pills, all counted and placed into little pill containers. I would, also, lay out the week for them: grocery shopping, outdoor activities, group activities to participate. My penchant for floating from place to place, thing to thing back then was extremely pronounced. Like most things in that part of my life, this job turned out to be pretty short lived; everything in my world — more or less — had about a six to seven-month shelf life before it expired, or I tired of it altogether.

One of my duties for that fine organization had been helping residents either move in or move out. Unlike other facilities where I held employment, there was no restriction on the amount of 'stuff' a resident could bring, yet there was a strict zero tolerance policy when it came to drinking or using illicit drugs on property. Often, how that played out was helping a prospective resident move an entire life's worth of belongings into a 3RD story unit: waterbed, entertainment center, player piano… only to have them relapse and drink about thirty-two hours later. And, back down the stairs with the piano, waterbed and everything else. In one-hundred-thirteen-degree summers, it became a bit much, and when the opportunity presented itself, I moved on.

****

My outlook on things, at that time, greatly improved. My perennial victim-hood of everything being someone else's fault, and my penchant for an endless fountain of pessimism had dried up; still, I felt a bit like a self-centered ten-year-old, prone to fits, outbursts, and hurling things when I would not to get my way in the most trivial of matters. Even then, days and moments would come along unexpected where I felt like something was clutching my ankles dragging me back down into the muck. I felt strongly and often that it was important that I not cry, *not for a moment… lest I may never be able to stop.*

****

I met Dr. Smith after I exited my job working with the war veterans and taken on another position in mid-town working with young adults in a long-term treatment setting that used throwback methodology from earlier days of treatment to provoke change within the clients. I think, at the time, it was called 'behavior modification' and was something I had been familiar with from previous experience. Whether wearing a small, handmade sign around your neck that states "DON'T TALK TO ME, I'M A LIAR" has its benefits or not is hard to say, but my experience was that it did not keep me sober.

From day one, I had some reservations as the program seemed to center around a morning ritual every day known as 'Circle.' A strong and exuberant personality was in charge, and circles could range anywhere from wildly comical to something close to public crucifixion, depending on what was going on, who was struggling, and the latest in a string of misbehaviors. The community was maybe fifteen young adults, a smattering from across the continent sent here for substance abuse issues, and most were really pretty good kids. A few times a week, Jerry, a contracted therapist came, an older, gentle and kind soul who seemed to be the grounding force of that place when things got a little bit crazy, which was about twice a week.

Joining him, and coming into the fold a bit later, was Dr. Peter Smith, a doctor who had been working with, and working on, something called bio-feedback for a number of years. As I mentioned before, his — what appeared to be pseudo-science — was greeted with a healthy and warm skepticism, although I found him to be a remarkably nice guy.

That said, I worked near his results: one woman, well, a girl had been a resident in this program for six months, and she demonstrated — what looked to be — severe problems in executive functioning. The things she said and did were usually wildly inappropriate, but it had the strange appearance that she simply could not help it. It was the way she was. Someone might mention the death of a loved one, and she would burst out laughing. Her name was Rosalee.

Three times a week, she would be pulled out of group, and go off with Dr. Smith to a small side room where he had an invitingly nice reclining chair. Near it was a computer with various electric-type boxes going in and out of it, some handheld video games, a set of headphones and a speedo swim cap with dozens of brightly colored wires coming out of it. And she would be wired up with the cap squarely upon her head, and just sit there and dawdle around, which he stared quizzically into a monitor that told a narrative of her brain activity and thought patterns. In a matter of weeks, the hard edges and lack of social graces began to smooth out in Rosalee, as I saw her whole affect begin to change behind his work.

I suppose it was a few months after this that I asked him if he thought he could work on me, away from my job. I still felt like my thinking was a country road sign full of bullet holes, trouble finishing sentences because I had trouble finishing thoughts. Attempts to try to focus, concentrate left me feeling as if hot steel was burning behind my forehead; multi-tasking was an impossibility.

I started to see this doctor, well, if you want to call him that. He was known for being raided periodically for running a pain clinic on the side which took no measure of ethics into consideration, as it turned out. But he seemed genuine in his interest to help me and the trouble I had with processing thoughts. A mild stimulant was prescribed, which I found I was intolerant. Odd, that having been a speed freak for a decade of my life, I could no longer handle the effects of a few cups of coffee or a small cup of cold medicine. It seemed to make my way of thinking very much worse. Peter did say we could do sessions at his eastside home on the weekends, and I was invited over the following Saturday to make a beginning.

Dr. Smith lived out on the eastside past my mom's place and the endless sprawl of suburbs that stretched across the desert floor where it meets the surrounding hills on all four sides. I had always hated the eastside, but in retrospect, because I was much younger, I hated a lot of things. I was the person who brought bad vibrations to the room, and then blamed the room for making me feel bad, such as it was.

It was a twenty-minute car ride, and Peter met me at the door, holding back a big, slobbering dog whilst he did so. Peter had perfectly straight white teeth and a schlock of grey hair that pegged him as being mildly mad-scientist-like. He invited me in and offered me a bottle of water, which I accepted.

I was offered a seat in a big and inviting leather chair that leaned back and sank in just enough to swallow a person like a giant fly trap. I sat back in the chair while Dr. Smith talked me through each move he made, first applying a number of small spots of an oily substance with a funny medical smell across different parts of my head. It reminded me of what you see pregnant women get during sonograms. It had a cool, slippery feel to it. Then, something like a speedo cap was tugged tightly down over my skull, and Dr. Smith had a series of wires of varying colors which he meticulously attached to multiple ports all over the swim cap. It felt tight and quite odd, and my cynicism certainly kicked in after a minute, I will admit; I felt completely ridiculous.

After having been greased and wired to perfection, Dr. Smith went about channeling this series of wires into a port on the other end of his PC computer. The system perked into life, with the hum and whir that computers had back then, as it noisily searched for a dial-up signal. Finally, a screen appeared with a series of glowing green graphs with zig zagging lines across them.

Peter gingerly placed a set of headphones over the cap, and a handheld video gaming device was placed in my hands, and I was encouraged to turn it on and play for a little bit; it might have been a Pokémon game, if memory serves, with a very dated interface. I turned it on, and sped my tiny avatar through a series of block mazes as the headphones came to life and intermittent patterns of beeps came through each ear at different times. I saw the glowing green screen come to life with spikes and dips on the graph that told a story, perhaps only understood by Dr. Smith himself. This went on for twenty minutes, maybe longer, before Peter finally turned to me and clasped his palms together exclaiming, "I think we're done for today!"

He went about trying to read the graph to me, showing me where my deficits were in terms of neural pathways. It has since been explained to me in greater detail that the brain operates much like a series of highways and state and local roads in a crowded metropolitan area. Sometimes, when the freeways and side roads are shut down, the brain will build a series of jacked up detours —

inefficient perhaps but functional — that then become worn. The signals we were giving the brain — my brain — were a series of prompts to open up some of those cleaner passageways, but it was hard to tell from where I sat. I felt a little tired, with several grease spots on my head, and none too optimistic about any results. But I went back every weekend for months.

It might have been after two months when Peter printed out these graphs and reviewed them with me, trying to explain in layman's terms what the spikes and dips meant, and most importantly, tracing the patterns that had changed since we had first began. I, of course, was unaware of it at the time, but I had begun to *think* in complete thoughts, small and simple pieces of cognition that would see themselves through to fruition. Up to that point, it was a daily occurrence to walk out to the mailbox and forget almost entirely why I stepped out the front door. Standing in the blazing sun with a puzzled frown on my face, I would march back inside to where a bowl of dry cereal still sat on the counter awaiting its pour of milk from several hours earlier. Things were very much like that back then.

But I went back week after week, as I had — what we call in the field — a partial scholarship. My tithing in the stake on mental health was about forty dollars an hour, and I brought that in-hand regularly for months to wear the wired swim cap and use the handheld device. The conditioning in my prior life made me skeptical. As someone who had consumed great deals of alcohol and other things, I always thought, "If I can't *feel* it, *it must not be working.*" Health restoratives, though, do not work on the same principles, as it should be. But slowly, maybe it was seven weeks or maybe it was ten, things began to open. The stressors of getting brain freeze when two or more tasks crossed my mind began to slip away. I enjoyed conversation much more, not straining to focus on what was being said.

As the weeks turned to months, that lifelong heavy blanket of frustration began to subside; what had felt like a lead apron of troubles and jumbled thoughts began to lift and I could *think clearly*. More profound was my new awareness of that fact that I had become extremely intuitive, a gift I had never known. After a life-long debacle of problems that reflected poor judgement and a lack of common sense, I seemed to take on a knack for solving problems, often seeming as if the solution to sometimes a cryptic and troublesome matter was hanging in midair, just waiting for me to grab it. I had become extremely intuitive about things and people, and no longer spoke in fragments of sentences and incomplete ideas. Things deep inside this globe of flesh were starting to re-arrange themselves, after decades of standing damaged.

I had begun, after all that time, to feel like a human being again.

SPEAK TO ME

I sit across from Tina, fidgeting with my hands, and yet struck by her grace. Beneath her head scarf is a shaved head from some sort of post-cancerous regimen, and yet at the same time, she radiates class and warmth from every pore — a true paramour and undiscovered movie star of some sort, a Joan Fontaine of modern times sitting in her art-filled studio lined with small but elegant ceramics and bold paintings, giving me some of her time.

****

I sought her out, well, *not specifically her* but help all the same, encumbered by old wounds that would not heal and stifled by what felt like a primeval reaction stuck deep down in the marrow of my central nervous system.

I cleaned up my life significantly in the past eleven years: my wardrobe was no longer a hodgepodge of old well-worn t-shirts and jeans; my vehicle was the nicest I ever owned; I went to the gym, and looked, well, *sober.* As it were, ten years passed since I had given up alcohol, and still, after all that time, I found myself cold, aloof. Sometimes just the presence of a crowd of people in a room felt like a razor had scraped my skin off; sound and light often seemed to have gone up a notch — some invisible knob turning sensory experience up to "intolerable." But those things, to me, were pretty livable, the types of things you learned to work around: wearing dark sunglasses helped, as well as looking at my phone for an imaginary emergency to, then, excuse myself from whatever group I happened to be in to attend to said situation. But what had brought me there, looking back, was not the bright lights, nor the dark imaginings that still troubled me far too often; nor was it the feverish nightmares of being hunted, or sinking into some hellish void. What made me make that initial call was proving to be a great interference in my long-term relationship with Jacquie, who stood by me for eight years. Simply put, I hated being touched. A casual brush of my would-be-spouse's arm felt like cobras crawling across my skin. It came and it went in varying degrees, but by and large, it was omnipresent — in bed, on the couch, in public. Intimacy — the real kind, the sharing of oneself with another — was a tricky thing and remains to be so today, to not back-up when that deeper level of connection to a human being presents itself. The double-edged sword was the chit chat and menial conversation to fill up the bandwidth in the room; it bores me, stifles me. It is not, and never has been, something for which I was naturally equipped; and yet, being called into real, heartfelt connection, talking about things of substance, made me want to run. At least, that was how I had always seen it. But it was that *cobra feeling*, wet snakes moving across my skin; that was what brought me.

I had been phoning a friend from Denver, Kevin, a therapist. We met at a gathering of some sober folks way up in the mountains west of Denver. He was bright, cynical and hilarious, as well as being extremely helpful. After some catching up around our respective careers, I told him — as vividly as I could describe — the difficulty I was having. I told him about feeling walled off, and the deep divide in our household, a crumbling structure which I could not seem to will myself out. He asked me, "Hey, what are you doing to fix that?"

I told him I had being using some meditation techniques I picked up along the way, some guided narrative types that, truth be known, helped some, but really having very little effect on the problem. "Dude," he started; Kevin always said dude. "You need professional help."

I felt the all-too-familiar dis-ease at the suggestion; I hated the cost, was not keen on discussing my childhood, and did not care much for the abrupt feeling of being left in mid-air after I did start to open up. Even working in the field of treatment and having seen time and again its benefits, I was not thrilled about doing therapy. And the cost, like I mentioned, was generally a hundred or so an hour, sometimes more. I had, in all fairness, my share of therapy. But I always insisted — deep within myself — that I was well, now; things were good, or at least better, which they were. I had long since recovered from the problems that ailed me — all the while unmindful of my own interior that seemed to suggest otherwise.

He asked me if I knew what EMDR was, and I confirmed I did. I recalled reading an article in a magazine about it twenty years prior. Whilst I might be a little inaccurate on the details, I think sometime in the mid-nineties, a therapist had been sitting in a public park, troubled by something, when she (or he) began watching a flock of birds fly back and forth in a horizontal pattern. As the story goes, she reports that it seemed to life whatever was, then, troubling her, and more or less, EMDR was born: using bilateral stimuli to unwind traumatic response, which all science seems to indicate, can become embedded in the nervous system.

Why I remembered that article was not the science, necessarily, as it was the stories that backed its validity: some guy had apparently been on the San Francisco bridge when it collapsed, the top roadway folding down onto the busy suspended roadway beneath, crushing dozens of motorists like insects. This particular survivor of the disaster could no longer function normally in every area of his life and sought out what, at the time, was unproven science, only to see benefit and great results. And it was this that I remembered: the earthquake story. I told Kevin that day I would, in fact, seek out some sort of help.

My finances that spring were in a shamble. I had taken on a side business on top of working in the treatment industry and would supplement having no capitol to run my small business with my regular take-home paycheck. The result was working eighty hours a week to balance the check book and find out month after month that I was losing my ass as a small business owner. As such, my foray into seeking out help was more of asking around and calling in a favor than the usual route of an internet search for therapeutic resources. Sometimes, knowing a few folks meant that you could call in a favor, and that was what I hoped to do then.

I called my friend, Eve, who I helped find employment when she moved to Arizona from New Mexico a couple of years prior. Eve was a brilliant young therapist, radiant and beautiful with some strong convictions about a host of subjects from politics to food choices. She was working at the Zen Institute at the time and had what seemed to be an overflowing ark of patients, but she told me that if I was open, I might be able to do some work with her mother, Tina. And that is how we met.

I called Tina a couple days later, and with some hesitation, told her a bit about what was going on: I hated being touched, sex had become troublesome, which all too often lead to a dreaded talk. At that point, any sort of intimacy was impossible. I, too, made mention that my finances were a mess, but I was needing the help. And with her cool, silky voice she always talked in, she told me that we would work together. Our arrangement was simple: we would meet at her house tucked away in the foothills of Tucson weekly, and I was to bring what I could; we would work until we were done. Some weeks, I would bring twenty dollars, some weeks forty, so on and so forth.

I remember thinking, when it got down to what was going to be necessary to sort myself out, I was extremely grateful my friend Eve — who I always had a quasi-crush on — had not taken me on as a client as much of my disclosure would probably be an unflattering event, if not a shameful one. One of my recent and favorite quotes to spout off to folks I worked with in the capacity of wellness was "at a minimum, alcoholism is very embarrassing," but

EMDR was a much deeper delve into the human soul, the disclosure of a hundred broken bones torched with gasoline.

We spent that first night, a warm spring evening nestled in the foothills overlooking that desert town, talking about my history. Rather than waste time, I took a deep breath and steeled myself for the point-blank sense of over-exposure, and went to some of the darker parts of my past: how I had a direct hand in burning my own house to the ground, how the animals left in my care did not survive, a car accident were my hand had been all but severed, a vicious beating that I had been part and parcel to, a few ugly odds and ends pieced together like some fragments of the warped puzzle that had been my early adult years.

"Well," she said with that wry grin, "The good news is... I don't think you are a sociopath." She explained the process of EMDR to me and pulled out a chart which I was shown. She recommended we set some targets. These were — as was explained to me — moments of things I remembered about an event, or sometimes things as simple as a symbol, something that signified an event in which I might have had a hard time remembering. She explained that from there, I was to visualize this 'target' or deeply unsettling event even though the image of what it was may shift, and let the EMDR do its work using bilateral stimulation with both light and sound, and allow the mind to reprocess what had occurred. Before we undertook the bilateral process, she would ask me for a number, on a scale of one-to-ten, how much that thought or event distressed me, and we would work over these things until that number dissipated, or at least went far down the scale.

I may not have mentioned, but I am a skeptic by nature, very deeply so, which always hovered somewhere between doubt or flat out cynicism of the unexplored; and this situation was entirely no different. However, as I often say, when someone reaches out for help, they do not necessarily always get to pick what that help looks like, which in this case was putting on a pair of dark goggles with a circular series of tiny lights and a cheap, older set of stereo headphones. Both were plugged into what appeared to be a small, stainless steel transmitter of some sort with a few dials on it.

I was urged to "take some deep breaths; relax." A barely audible low hum from the small machine kicked on, and a synchronized dance of artificial red lights began to drag my attention back and forth — left, then, right. The pitch coincided perfectly with those lights, dragging my attention to left, then, right. I sat there, amused, cynical, but fully committed to whatever unanticipated event was to happen next.

"Now, tell me about target number one," she said. So, I did.

****

Joel and I had been driving on Easter Sunday. We took Joel's girlfriend Janine's car all the way out to the eastside to say hello to my mom, catch a meal of some sort, rest assured, and likely — back then — borrow a few bucks, usually about twenty. My life was perpetually falling forward into adulthood yet marred by irresponsibility; we were always broke and always looking for a little something extra. A couple of hungry ghosts committed to — if nothing else — a good time. Shortly after pulling out of my mom's driveway, we smoked the last of our pot — just a fraction of a fraction, not nearly enough to make a difference. We headed back downtown toward Joel's little adobe studio, where we spent a lot of afternoons winding through elaborate sarcasms and listening to records nobody had ever heard.

I had my window rolled down, the warm spring wind rushing into the car. A dirty Converse Chuck Taylor rested itself up on the dash, my arm outside the window with my hand on the roof tapping out the drum section of some heavy rock as we pulled onto the ramp that drops us down onto Aviation Highway, a quick little stretch of road that shoots you from the southeast side straight into downtown and named, presumably, for the fact that it lies right under the flightpath of planes landing at both the nearby air force base and the small but efficient airport I was to use many, many times later on.

As soon as we merged, we were shot down into the normal high trajectory traffic that bulleted down that roadway. I began to laugh and make commentary on the older white service van a few paces ahead in the right lane, who — clearly — had started his celebration of Christ having done some hard drinking early. The guy was all over the road, his ailing Ford van pitching left and then right as the lines struggled to contain him; his driving was clearly reckless and alcohol-fueled, and both our vehicle and his were going upwards of seventy miles per hour. I made comment on it, but I cannot remember what I said. Joel sped up and went to pass when the driver swung wildly to the left and veering into our lane. Joel grabbed the wheel and jerked it to the left. We hit the curb, a tin can in flight, for a moment.

Something often portrayed in film — though not entirely inaccurate — is that finite point in time when the pressing of impending danger turns fractions of seconds into what feels like molasses. When every fiber, every nerve, every muscle turns to brittle glass, the unusual sense of being catapulted into flight creeps by; and in the face of real powerlessness, you brace yourself as the moment begins narrating the next portion of the story, all on its own.

A thunderclap of metal hitting concrete fills our ears, and a blizzard of broken glass sprays me in the face. I am not sure, but I believe I am screaming. We tumble to a stop — upside down — necks twisted in a vertical heap, limbs splayed everywhere. The sounds of a few lazy and discarded car parts rolling away before settling to rest on the roadway gives way to absolute and stunning silence.

"Oh shit! Holy shit!" I say, before a very natural sense to escape quickly and crawl out of the crushed cabin takes hold. I am a skinny kid, more so than Joel, and with very little effort, I crawl out. The sun is shining, and I am free. I pace in circles, the back wheel of the Datsun lazily spinning. The other car that had been in our cluster of commuters — a Mercedes — makes a U-turn. The van — in the distance now — slows, then roars off. The Mercedes parks and a lovely blonde woman in a mink coat gets out, looking elegant but perhaps over dressed for a hot spring afternoon. Joel crawls across the pavement breathing heavy, having freed himself from the wreck. He stands up. He stares at me blinking, and his jaw drops.

Something is happening with his face... No, not injured, but a look I have not seen him make ever before.

I go to run my fingers through my hair, and I am splashed abruptly, and I am wet, which seems strange. I look, puzzled, at a hand spinning around on a thread of skin, and a jet of bright red blood sparing yards in the air, something that would later be medically described as "de-gloved" has pulled the skin into a sagging mess, like a sock that has had the wrong thread pulled, rendering it fit for the waste can.

The Mercedes woman tries to help. Joel is trying to help. His panic is making me panic. I cuss a lot. A very real sensation, not of pain but of thirst, takes over... as pints, perhaps quarts by this point, of blood go un-replenished. My throat is a parched and rainless plain. I beg for water. A circle of faces stare down, and I hear a siren in the background. An uncomfortable and disjointing series of faces hover over; I feel straps and the sensation of being moved as the surrounding sea of faces shuffles me into the back of an ambulance.

****

In the telling of this to Tina, I know very little, a memory of a memory, a shadow of a moment in time, cast off and lost to me. The lights dance back and forth. She asks, "What is your level of discomfort of these thoughts? Scale of one-to-ten, please." I find the question to be quite obtuse, so I make a number up. "Seven."

I press myself to try to remember further. I try to summon up the horror of that day but cannot get an accurate read on it. I sit there, in that warm studio, looking like a poorly executed science fiction movie, decked out in laser goggles and headphones, drifting into skepticism, the accident slipping further from me, despite my efforts to retrieve it. I know now, in that process, there is no need to go looking for it... because it will come find you.

I sat there when a peculiar and distinct smell hit my nostrils. I flickered briefly, wondering if perhaps something in the room had caught fire, but the smell, while not unpleasant, was not a burnt smell, but a smell I have known before, exactly one time in my life.

****

I jolt awake. I am in the hospital. It feels like it is midnight. The room is barely lit, a few muted lights along the baseboards, and the soft glow of a heart monitor that pulses with some regularity. The soft beeps and chirps of monitoring equipment provides its own quiet chorus, and I am alone. Brown dried blood is smeared across my hospital gown in few paint strokes, and my arm is a think wad of hospital bandage with a few clear lines of fluid protruding. A nasal cannula is pulled over my ears, jetting small puffs of cool oxygen up my nose. Four dull bulbs flicker at the end of each finger on my right hand.

The couple of hours I was awake before then, conscious of this quiet darkness, had been excruciating; I remember begging the medics for morphine, maybe not so much to cut the pain as to cut the reality of what had happened. They refuted, and said I would have to wait until we got to the hospital and see what the surgeon wanted to do. I laid there a little while, writhing around in my bed, before a nurse came to prep me; she positioned a small cloth that dropped down, separating me from my injury, at least, in the visual sense.

"This… will hurt," she said, then added, "Whatever you do, don't look." I felt a blowtorch of incredible pain — beyond anything — shoot up my right arm. And maybe I should not have, but I did; I did look.

She turned my hand around in a wash bin, folding it in the opposite direction up against my arm, and took some sort of scrub brush and was scrubbing at road grit, and the two bloody severed ends rinsed with iodine. I saw what appeared to be a white light and uttered a scream I never made before as the pain threshold of what any human could stand was broken through.

A sedative was administered, but my screaming continued.

"15 CC more, stat!" The nurse says to the assistant trying to manage me. My screams turn to a blur of fading consciousness, and the blackness scoops me up, pulling me deep into its fold. And when I come to, it is dark and quiet. The machines that monitor my heartbeat begin to pick up pace, and in volume. I am starting to panic when an orderly comes in to check on things.

"Your family is here… Would you like to see them now?" she asked, and I obliged. Up to that point, I screamed; I begged for morphine; I bit my lower lip twisting around on the gurney; I even might have prayed. But when my mom walked into that room, so dark and quiet, for the first time that day, I began to cry.

The next morning, after I came out from a fog of Dilaudid and sedative, I was wheeled downstairs into another section of the hospital where I was outfitted with something from the rehabilitation specialists. I sat there, thoughts hovering in the room, before I was brought back to a room, shelved with solvents and sheets of different medical materials rolled up nearby.

****

I smelt that smell, that warm vinyl smell of a piece of light blue plastic as it is being heated up and soaked in a vat of... of something, about to be wrapped like a plastic encasement around my injury, snugly holding everything in place. It would become my companion for the next year or so, yet I had forgotten this detail **entirely**... never thought one iota about it since its departure back in 1992. And yet, there I sat, in that leather seat, a few modest wires stemming from the glasses that blinked with Christmas-like regularity from my face, absorbing a hospital smell I had not thought of, nor remembered in years. But... it was there.

I took the glasses and headphones off and placed them in my lap. "That was...weird." I said, followed by, "Something most definitely just happened." Tina asked what and I told her about that bit, the smell and tapping into that, how it just jumped up through me.

"Yes," she nodded. "That's what this does."

****

The weeks and handful of months following the accident were a grotesque and stunning epilogue in human anatomy and terrible visions. These were the real-life things that haunted my dreams as a kid, that compelled me as a young teenager, whose mind fixated on some dark imaginary nether region of suffering, its brushstrokes cast in hues of deep blue.

My arm had blown up to about the size of my thigh and was an oozing and juicy mess, a bloated and unsightly appendage wrapped in a sterile medical sock from which my fingers protruded, dull and lifeless. My appetite had taken to the hills as I could never bring myself to eat more than a bite or two of food, wildly nauseated at my own condition, and even more so from the ensuing recovery from it. Nights turned into a strange and horrible experiment where, as I dozed off to medicated sleep, I would feel — *truly **feel*** — my fingers snapping to some rhythm of their own accord, or feel myself make a flicking motion with my thumb and forefinger, only to look down at the same fingers, drab and immobile as they sent false signals, former imaginations from functions in previous years. I would lie awake many of those nights, staring at my hand. Visitors came almost every day, telling me how fortunate and lucky I was, though I felt anything but. Truthfully, something happened — and had been explained to me — of which had some significance that I would not digest on any kind of level, let alone a spiritual level, for many years to come.

The insurance adjuster assigned to investigate the injury on his company's behalf — who made a simple and basic living mitigating circumstances under which large pay outs might be owed — had been bedside just a couple of weeks prior. He was a nice enough guy, asked some basic questions about the accident, though he already had a good picture of the event having talked to the driver, my friend Joel. He did his due diligence, nonetheless, and asked me about the white van, how fast we were going, the basics. He, then, asked a simple question: "Were you wearing a seatbelt?"

In truth, no. No, I had not had a seatbelt on. My mind began to whirl with an answer because — I suspected intuitively — it would probably greatly affect the outcome of what came next. But, before I could answer, the agent seemingly answered his own question, based on probability and past statistics: "Of course, you were. Wearing a seatbelt, that is. Vehicles travelling over 65 miles an hour in a multiple rollover situation are always thrown from the vehicle." I pictured for a moment what he was saying. The very real idea that basic physics suggested I should have been pitched halfway out the window before succumbing to the weight of the vehicle myself. It gave me pause. The basic, well, miracle of what had happened would go unrecognized for many years.

****

I wanted, maybe needed, to be done with that for the night, so we reviewed some targets we set, and organized the things we had identified that needed much sorting through. Some are things I personally could never nor would never expose to the world, in published form. On a one-to-one level, perhaps. We set an appointment to meet the following Thursday night; I got in my truck, and headed home.

When I returned, Tina was in a bright flowing gown, again, with a silk headscarf, and invited me in for a glass of water infused with mint. Some of the artwork in her studio had been shuffled around, and a large hound, nearly waist high, let out a groan and wagged its tail, probably a meek gesture of its younger self who would jump any visitor coming in the door. She opened up a cabinet and pulled out the file we started working on together, my file, as it were.

****

I used to run with these guys; they played in a band, which seemed to loan credence to my adaptation of some sort of street personality; looking back, that — for a while — was what I wanted and needed to be, and something about the practicing of being a deviant, turns into the real thing after a time. Musically, I did a few loud and caustic things myself, though honing any real musical ability would not become a facet of my life for another two decades. But the real juice, the real kick, was getting to be in the inner circle of a group of guys, well-known, extremely talented and well-liked. Most buildings they played in in those perilous years through the mid-nineties were usually packed. When I departed from mom's house, it was them that I took up residence with in a mustard yellow captain's house, flanked by tiny cottages in a busy university neighborhood. The living room housed this massive black drum kit and Marshall Amplifiers that filled the room and made you feel like your head might explode, even when they were turned off. The window dressing of our lives was that of most young and irresponsible bachelor types: recycled butter containers used as cereal bowls, a random fork or spoon laying around, armfuls of condiments taken from whatever nearby food establishment had been relieved of them, dirty carpets, mattresses on floors.

Our house was a parade of visitors at all hours, and all hours were kept. I stayed in an adjoining laundry room, decent in size and perhaps more so because it lacked a washer and dryer. An old gas water heater kept me company, shaking and boiling and rattling a great deal of the time. Most days, it seemed like it would explode at any minute, which I did my best to make peace with. One day — in permanent magic marker — I pained a large smiling face across the side of the cylinder, and it remained that way, a smiling stick of dynamite, shaking and rattling periodically.

We had this neighbor, a very sweet and mild older gentlemen who owned a small yard upkeep service who drove an army green Datsun pick-up truck. He asked a number of times over the months to "keep it down," one time with tears in his eyes. I do not think we meant to be noisy, nor was it our intention to be bad neighbors... we just seemingly had the inability to do anything other than make a terrific racket. Even with the eggshell foam lining the inside of the house, it was just simply a ten-decibel house. If memory serves, that guy actually borrowed some of the extra foam we had, not to keep his noise in, but to keep our noise *out*.

Every night, we would ride our bikes to various gigs happening around town, or we piled in my El Camino to go find out where a bunch of drinking would be going on. Sometimes, the touring bands would come over late after their headlining gigs, and just come hang with us. There was this Canadian band I grew up listening to, DOA. One time, they came over and smoked and drank a bit. For a young man who drifted in and out of darkness, who had fits of deep depression, strange dreams and tumultuous demons clawing at his back, it was actually a good time to be alive.

I dreamt, among other things, of the ocean a great deal back then. Some strange, murky-green inner space where things squirmed, and giant monoliths of toothed-fish swam through my subconscious. I became, as it were, a bit obsessed with the idea of marine life, and decided with all the flimsy muster of a guy with no other plans to be a marine biologist, only one who did not attend school nor took any of the active steps a normal person might consider who was on a trajectory for a doctorate level degree. I settled, in the end, for scuba diving classes in a swimming pool, which was to be followed by a summer trip to Himalaya Playa, a quick and brief disastrous outing fueled by one large, brown box full of warm quarts of Mexican beer. My shoes and all my other clothes went out with the tide that weekend when Joel — who accompanied me — and I had a late-night argument. I kicked the side of the tent we were stationed at, and stormed off down the beach, but much closer to the tide to get some sleep. I woke up underwater a few hours later.

The dive trip, and later, a quick trip to San Diego, were funded by a pinnace I received from the car accident, a gesture from the insurance policy in which only liability insurance was held that I would be okay; and for a while, I was.

The San Diego trip, which was Rick, Joel and I, was good. We got to the beach at around 5:00am and played in the surf as the sky of greys opened up into a brilliant California morning. On a whim, we headed to Sea World. I was fascinated as a young kid being there. I remember a moment, looking down in a tiny pool, and seeing the slightest of hammerhead sharks, maybe a foot-long swimming past. I remember being so fascinated, as my family kept the plodding pace with the crowd, moving from sight to sight, being transfixed, before ultimately becoming separated from them; and I remember my mother finding me, eyes filled both terror and relief, when I was finally retrieved, though I was none the wiser. I was still staring hypnotically at that small pool.

Our experience, this ill-fitted and street punk trio, proved to be both comic and perilous, as if some magnetism to a natural chaotic order of things pulled us from event to event, though the subterfuge that followed came all at my own prompting, which, looking back, it usually did.

We had been smoking on that little sky carriage that crawled across the top of the park, looking down at the park below and offering a stunning view of San Diego. Rick did his absolute best to try and rock the cart and topple us to death, which did not happen, and I did not enjoy. I was not much for heights.

When we finally landed at the adjoining bridge where you disembark the ride, I said, "Hey. What about the killer whales? Let's go see those." We zig-zagged through the park, bumping through the traffic of every sort holding dolphin balloons with sunscreen and floppy hats and kids in tow.

Unmindful of anything that resembled staying on schedule, we walked into a packed stadium with some sort of killer whale show well underway. The few remaining seats were not good ones: three vinyl plastic chairs pressed up against the glass, with likely the poorest view from any vantage point of the carefully trained and orchestrated magic that came from training, confining and coercing these magnificent creatures. Looking back, we were ground zero "splash zone" participants, staring at the cool, glass screen of blue water where, on occasion, a field of black would bullet past and the occasional waterfall of salt water drenched us.

The arena went quiet after a while, and I was quick to tire of almost anything that was in front of me suddenly failed to stimulate. "Well, let's go," I remarked. The quiet of the arena and onlookers was broken up by what might have been a snare drum roll, hard to say for sure. We stood up near that glass, looking around for an exit. Rather than fight our way through the narrow aisle of seats pressed against the glass, I pointed to a short cut: a long ramp full of shifting shallow water to get to the north exit on the other side.

We took off our sandals and jumped up on ledge and stepped on to the ramp and treaded through the few inches of water. Mayhem ensued! Screaming! "Get down," or maybe, "Get back!" Lots of ruckus. Perplexed at all the yelling, I looked around at a few frantic park employees barking directions… at us. Turning my head to the right, I could see on the massive jumbo Tron, upward of forty feet high, Rick, Joel and myself, standing in water, our images cast thirty feet high. The drum roll halted, and like a powerful locomotive, this giant black fish leapt from the water, and was sliding up at us. In truth, it was the first good look I got at a killer whale since arriving there, staring into those powerful jaws at the pink wagging tongue, its wide, deep sea-smile propelling us backwards into maelstrom; and we tumbled off the platform, falling backwards in the chairs with an entire audience shouting boos and hisses from an obstructed view and a meltdown in the ninth inning of, what turned out to be, a lousy finish.

"One more move like that, and the three of you are banned for life from the Park," a security guard snapped at us. We wandered off, the remainder of the day, uneventful.

The drive back to Tucson was pockmarked by dust storms and stifling heat in Joel's Corolla whose air conditioner met an early expiration date; we took off our shirts and were soaking them with bottled water, hanging them between the doors and chassis, wet curtains that flapped madly around providing some, but not much, relief. As the sun set and we pulled into the home stretch, we got a panoramic view of our local mountain range burning mightily. A staple of Arizona fires was then, and may still be, always punctuated by out of control wild fires of biblical proportion. Coupled with the heat, it provided its own nary welcome: *come join us back in hell.*

A few days after returning, this young hellion, Mike, caught Rick on the street and passed along to him a handbill for a house party; we always travelled in numbers, too. Mike was not in our scene, not really. Mike and his friends of fourteen or fifteen guys had their own look: pegged pants, Fred Perry shirts, red suspenders and shaved heads. They fancied themselves a working-class street gang modeled after some scene that had erupted in Britain in the 1960s, though I was never convinced any of them actually worked. The party we were invited to was at Mike's house, tucked among a of group of twelve or so identical casitas right off of Ninth Street and was advertised as having a couple of kegs of beer, and a three dollar cover. Sounded reasonable.

Mike and his friends were brawlers, pack animals that looked for the weak, before somehow taking fault or offense at some imaginary indiscretion of those they had targeted. They were known, simply, as a group of guys who tended to beat others to a bloody pulp. That said, while we were cut from a different cloth, Rick had a lot of weight in these large overlapping circles of musicians. People naturally wanted to size-up to him and be his friend; he had charisma like that. Even with his wildly angled (broken) nose and odd features, Rick had an innate grit of humor, caustic sarcasm and over the top personality, a natural people magnet.

We had not been at Mike's too long that night, maybe an hour or two, before trouble had started. A friend we knew, a guy who hung out of the periphery, was asked to step outside by Mike — friends in town — to get some boots. Backpedaling as this group started to circle like pack animals, gearing up for a fight, Joel wandered out in the alley — maybe to take a piss, maybe to get some air — and his natural, happy-go-lucky personality got involved.

"Hey guys, lets cool this one out. Everything is cool man. Let's just have a good…" And before he could finish the sentence, a full bottle of beer crashed across his face, spilling bright red blood on the ground. The initial and intended target saw his chance to run, and hightailed it down the alley at full speed, before Joel crumpled to the ground as fists and bottles rained down on his head.

It was barely a handful of minutes later, Mike stood there talking to Rick, apologizing profusely through a half drunken blur: "We did not know he was with you. We're sorry man. This was a huge mistake."

Rick put a finger in his face: "This isn't over, Mike. We'll settle this later." Half the group saddled up and took Joel to the emergency room to get a few dozen stitches to sew up the flap of forehead that hung over his left eye; the other half of guys went back to the house, tense, worried, and angry.

Joel returned from the emergency room, and the bulk of us had been up all night drinking, talking and playing cards. Joel was a mess: several good-sized knots circling the globe of his head as if boll weevils had taken nest there; his ribs a dark array of bruises, a Picasso of deep purples and blues and yellows taking shape like a continental map. "Ah man… it hurts," he said, touching his forehead. By that point, it was 5:30, the sun lurched far in the horizon, and Rick stood up looking around the room with a coy gaze.

"Well," he said, "how do you want to handle this? My vote," he added, "is we just handle it right now."

We loaded up in the El Camino: Mark, Joel, Rick, Eddie and me. Joel was holding a baseball bat, Rick a lead pipe. We drifted up Euclid with three friends in the bed of the Camino before turning into the alley where the soft crunching of tires and gravel was met by the only other sound of a few solitary birds giving praise to the morning. We parked and the tick of the engine fell silent under that quiet, pink, desert sky and made our way up the alley.

We walked onto Mike's porch, and the window was open; we could hear an oscillating fan blowing air back and forth. Plastic red cups, cigarette butts and the sour, warm smell of ferment hung around the porch. Rick took the butt end of the piece of plumbing pipe he was holding and banged loudly on the flimsy door, cracking it. Silence.

He banged a second time, and then placed his hand on the doorknob. It turned, unlocked from the night before. He swung it open, and again, complete stillness, save for the oscillating fan doing its work.

Mike sat up in bed, his narrow frame marked by a couple of small hand done tattoos, in white fruit of the loom underwear on a mattress with sheets thrown about on the ground. He rubbed his eyes and nervously croaked, "Um… what's up guys?" as the first blow from a piece of steel pipe cracked him squarely across the cheekbone.

"Your turn now!" Rick bellowed, as a flurry of swings from the bat and pipe pinned him in the corner. He was screaming.

Mark ripped the phone out of the wall and kicked over the television set. He took the small white fan, and broke it against the doorway; he stomped his combat boot through the coffee table as Eddie looked for anything remotely of value that he could take for the haul, at least anything Mark had not already broken.

The sound that echoing thump of steel meeting bone continued; I looked across the doorway at the lump of flesh Mike had become: shins and arms nearly broken from holding them up to fend of the beating, his shrieks having fallen into a silent gurgle.

I can only convey that the horror that came over me was akin to, perhaps, the first viewing of the Rodney King take oh-so long ago before it lit up that warm beachside metropolis in flames and hurled brick.

Only this was here, and it was now.

I swallowed hard, and panic shot through me like a hot wire. I had never seen — nor wanted to see — someone murdered, but in my vivid imagination which had always been acutely sensitive to violence, I imagined it looked a great deal like this. And, it had always been that way, ever since I was a kid. Anything I witnessed, I could feel the knife or the bat, feel my teeth being drilled into without Novocain, or slide into the role of an animal in a cage, its cage marked and labeled 'For Vivisection.'

"Stop," I said lowly, then much louder. "You guys…stop! You're killing him." The pipe and bat flung aside; we turned to bolt and Mike was an unsightly twist of limbs and fading consciousness. We turned to go, and Joel turned back to him, a storm of fists raining down on Mike's head who was light years beyond mounting a defense any further. I grabbed Joel's wrist, my panic having risen to full boil. *Oh God. Dear God, don't let him be dead. Dear God.*

We fled, this tsunami group of street urchins having settled a score quickly in a staggering display of violence.

****

Weeks later in the process, I posed this question to Tina: "So, when do you think we'll be done? How long, exactly, is this supposed to last?" to which she turned kindly back on me.

"Oh, I won't know when you are done, but I bet you will."

And the timing of that, it turned out, was odd. That week I attended a small backyard function hosted by some old friends of mine. Walking in the door, I was greeted by Jessica, who I had not seen in maybe eight months. "Hey you!" she shouted, and stepped up giving me a big hug. The sensation of that hug was warm and bright, a delightful squeeze that made me feel safer right away, no venom and no darkness to speak of. Matters in my central nervous system, really, in my soul, had been set straight.

I hugged her back, "It's good to see you, too. It really is."

CHANNELS

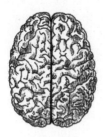

Up the street from my house in Dallas is a busy intersection, running east beneath a toll road. Everyday around 5:00pm, it is a snare of traffic, dozens of cars deep probing each way and aggressively punching their way through the yellow lights that flicker to red. I am there with them, often. I stop sometimes to look around at my fellow commuters, some talking on their phones, some gripping the steering wheel wringing out the stressors of the day.

On the telephone wires a couple of stories up, a gathering of birds of various sorts congregate every day — hundreds if not thousands — in some sort of impromptu social gathering only understood by them. This has steadily become my favorite part of the day, to roll down my windows and hear the chatter of this splendid winged symphony giving one last salute to a sun fading in a golden canvas swathed in birdsong. Most of the others seem to take no notice at all. It is a gift I stumbled upon, connecting me back to the present moment.

****

I sit quietly, taking deep breaths, engaging a simple practice that
— time and again — eluded me, and yet is something worth
striving. The static energy of a hundred tiny problems races
through my mind: bills, emails, tasks at work, a teeth-grinding
accumulation of needling thoughts, unsettling and frustrating.

I take three more deep breaths, straightening my spine into
perfect form, palms open, waiting to feel, *truly feel,* this buildup
of frustration pass, and let my energy drop back into my limbs. I
breathe; I wait; I relax. It takes a few minutes, and I resume my
effort, waiting and breathing; for soon, I will arrive, again, on the
couch I sit, a few birds outside, a dog barking off in the distance,
the hum of the air conditioner, all pulling me back into the room,
quiet and awake, here in the present. I become worry-less and
optimistic, but like yesterday and the day before, it takes a lot of
work to get here.

This, outside of a nice grind on whatever happens to be my
favorite coffee as of late, is how I start my mornings: getting quiet,
asking for guidance and inspiration, and taking in deep, heavy
breaths until the gathering storm-clouds of thoughts and worry
fall away, and a clarity and presence takes over.

****

I had a therapist — her name was Gabrielle — tell me once
that I carried all of my energy in my head, that when something
unsettling came — which, in my world, was likely to be just about
anything at all — I would rush up into my head to sort things
out. That sounded like an abstract and obtuse idea, added to a few
others she had already put on my plate. She mentioned something
about an "inner child" weeks before, to which I bristled with
cynicism and brushed off altogether.

On this point though, it struck me as odd that she made
that declaration about me pushing my energy up into my head;
furthermore, at that time, I did not know what she meant about
the summary she had so eloquently given me… until about a
week later. I was talking to a business acquaintance, Tom, tall and

friendly, a guy I knew from a number of places I used to frequent. He was the clinical supervisor at a small, psychiatric hospital on the northwest side of Tucson, and as a person, he was as harmless as a church mouse. All things considered, I liked Tom and was always happy to see him. So, I was surprised that in the course of a general five-minute conversation, I found myself completely tense as if waiting for him to strike me blindly with an open fist. I saw my mind race for an excuse to cut the conversation short: *maybe I could fabricate needing to make an important call or use the restroom; maybe I could conjure a business lunch for which I was running a bit late.* Except, I was *aware of it.* And in that funny way that consciousness often expands, I realized: this was nothing new. I felt this way, far too often, in far too many situations: leaning into a wind that was not blowing, every fiber in my body turning to glass and waiting to be shattered, hatching an escape plan from even the most mundane and simplest of human contact.

I realized, finally, what Gabrielle had been trying to say, and in our next conversation, I offered a full report on *watching,* truly observing, the nature of my thought-life as I moved about in seemingly ordinary situations.

It was then, I think, that I began a journey within a journey. By that time, I had a bit over twelve years of sobriety time, and the trappings and successes of my life might have camouflaged that on the interior; except, I felt messy, unkempt, and often stricken with thoughts that felt like a nuclear reactor leaking toxic fluid from its hull. Of course, thoughts of extreme violence would come and go, and always had; these, coupled with the tension I carried that was constructed of uncertainty became something I can only describe as a lack of **SAFETY** at times, and immobilizing.

****

I take three deep breaths, yearning and eager to return to wherever my hands and feet are, wherever my body is. It is here, in presence, in this moment, packed into my own life-force, that I am safe, perhaps always have been. It might be wherever I am currently planted — on a seat or standing on a piece of asphalt. It takes vigorous effort that feels not at all like holding on, but rather, a *letting go*, which in a way, is the harder of the two tasks.

On this note, it occurs to me quite often, for all the discord I create, for all of the dark imaginings I project as being in my near future, almost none of these prove to have any bearing on reality whatsoever. As an example, I can say, for all of my worries over the past fifteen years or so, not once have I been late on a bill or payment; not once have I gone hungry nor ran out of gas. Of infinite possibilities of calamity *that could* happen, in practice, almost none of them ever actually do. I have, however, been embarrassed on occasion, but the humility found in those lessons, looking back, became an asset. In this, I have found perception to be everything. I try — as often as possible — to return my thoughts to my hands and feet, to bring my thoughts back to where I am standing, to bring my thoughts back to the present. This requires constant work, but I have found this to be wholly worthwhile.

****

There are volumes and volumes of books which will capture, in greater detail, practices of mediation and calming the mind — transforming both thoughts and perception — than this one. That said, I feel I would do my readers — some of whom may have, also, suffered head injuries and issues resulting from that — a disservice if I did not offer the technique I found to be a great resource in not only surviving myself but also helping me to flourish and thrive, such as I have over the past twelve or so years. These things are not so much practices as they are daily disciplines, labors of the spirit. Getting well and getting healthy was never an easy job; and something else I found to be true of this life: nothing worthwhile is simply given over for free. Progress, in any medium, comes with practice, patience and work. That said, there is a saying I often hear: "take what you want and discard the rest." I hope some of this information will serve you, as it has I.

My thinking these days — whilst greatly healed from its prior state — is still prone to summoning nightmarish visions from time to time. For years, the impact of my own darkness into my humanity felt a bit like getting hit by a train. I might be standing in the kitchen, maybe in a crowded room, when a very real sensation or thought of bones snapping like twigs, or of immense harm, would overtake me. The result would be — what I liken to — that of an ice cream headache: a wincing burst of intolerable thought which would come suddenly as my spine grows stiff and my jaw clenches up, usually leaving me shaken for the next couple of hours doubting my sanity and turning into this great ill-kept secret that, perhaps, I do not think like a 'normal' person should. I came up with, what I call, an 'invitational mediation,' which has helped me greatly.

When these thoughts occur, rather than push them back or question my sanity becoming grave and morose like I have a million times before, I stop. I take three or four deep, centering breaths and I say, "Welcome," or sometimes "Please come in," inviting whatever darkness arrives. I wait a few seconds, in a cerebral pause of sorts, and rather than feeling as if I have been run over by a train, I feel more like something *has blown through me,* a dark and malevolent force created by damaged neural pathways that ultimately passes as quickly as it showed up. In this, I have learned I must face my own darkness squarely, as I let it pass through, rather than dwell on it; and Reader, it always does. It will always pass.

****

Before going further, I ought to explain I lead a busy, busy life. Every day is a composite of nodding to return e-mails, take care of the pets, prioritizing a to-do list that grows exponentially rather than retracting to what — mentally — would appear to be a manageable amount, high-stress and high-pressure situations that arise out of a long standing tenure in the field of substance abuse and mental health. The nature of my work, at times, demands a cool hand; often, people's lives depend upon a judgement call or a decision I must make — in the moment usually — without time to contemplate it. And in this, I am not different from most folks: we all lead busy lives; we all have things to do, and goals we are trying to accomplish.

I find, under duress, the first thing to go is my patience; the second thing to depart is my tact in dealing with whatever I have grown impatient. When it begins to feel like "I have too many programs running" upstairs, agitation sets on quick, and I have a strong talent for making myself — and those around me — a bit miserable; and whatever was happening before what suddenly came on is usually still unresolved after the bout of frustration anyway.

Considering this, most days, I sit down, and this is my practice: a visualized and premeditated contemplation of both peace and success, no matter how small the details. I find a spot where I can sit in sustained comfort for about twenty minutes, usually my favorite spot in the house that carries an inherent sense of safety. I make sure my body is relaxed, calm, but not in a slouched position. I sit, breathing deeply, repeatedly, until I feel my thoughts and central nervous system stop buzzing, and wait for what feels like my energy gently dropping down into my body, my hands and feet; I wait until my mind is nearly clear, though this is not always an easy task, and I begin visualizing my day.

I see myself getting up from the couch and going to the refrigerator for breakfast; I visualize myself making a healthy choice. I, then, play the day forward ever so slightly visualizing myself driving to my first task of the day, and the traffic snare that inevitably follows. In this, I see myself inviting other motorists (who would ordinarily warrant a nasty response) to cut into the merging lane with a polite wave. I say, out loud, "Help me to be calm and peaceful, kind to those who come across my path." I see myself walking into the office with a genuine and sincere greeting to those already there — *especially* with whom I have personality clashes with regularly. I see myself opening emails, which may sometimes contain three pieces of good news and four pieces of bad news; I visualize grace, humility, and a quiet heart to address those emails, taking whatever problems the day has brought me in quiet stride. I see the parts of my day where I ordinarily register complaint — "I'm so tired of this shit," or "He really never takes his duties that seriously" — and I see myself remaining quiet in the face of these things. Again, I may ask: "Help me to be quiet today."

After mentally addressing what I believe will be the content of my day, I say what might be considered an additional request "to be fitted to deal with the things I simply cannot foresee, whatever they might be." Believe it or not, I do this, every day. It has served me well over the years.

Other times, I find simply sitting quietly with this Power which saved me a wretched ending fits me perfectly, calm and quiet times when I can get in touch with each tendon, each nerve ending, each passing thought, marveling at the facts of life itself. It is on these days I affirm — out loud — everything I can think of to be grateful. Always included on this list — not just the successes and accolades — are the failures as well, these things which taught me great resilience. In fact, I make it a regular practice to wish for, pray for and hope for hardship.

I do not believe — not even for one second — that the act of doing this *creates hardship,* but rather, places me in perfect alignment when trouble comes. In times like those, I can look back and think, "Yes, I asked for this. Now, it is here; it teaches me lessons that I otherwise could not be taught." In doing so, I learned — repeatedly — to lean into my life rather than flee from it.

****

Lastly, I have found, over years of study, the most powerful of all restorative aids, the greatest medicine ever known to mankind, is the simple belief that one can get well; for after all, a thousand placebo study tests in a laboratory could not possibly be flawed, could they? But, while hope and belief will gain one much, healing needs a means and a route, a path to wellness, if you will.

I have read in the dozens simple stories of guided meditations being deployed to cure a wide spectrum of ailments. Not so long ago, I was listening to a workshop given by Carolyne Myss, a self-styled mystic with an eloquent and profound way of talking on matters of the spirit. In this recorded lecture, she makes mention of a boy she had known with a brain tumor that was overgrown and considered to be inoperable by the medical team assigned to treating him. The family sought non-surgical means to remedy his grave and likely fatal tumor: each morning, he would sit and imagine fighter pilots in small spaceships cruising through outer space and aiming their lasers and missiles at a giant, fleshy orb floating in blank space. This sphere, as it were, was the tumor tucked away in the grey matter of his brain. He called it "Planet Meatball." And in this young boy's imagination, each day the spaceships would take to task launching missiles into his fleshy exterior, until one day, it came to him in his vison: the meatball exploded into dust. On his next doctor's visit, it was found that no trace remained of the tumor that was destined to kill this child.

It had not occurred to me until far later to utilize such imagery and working vision to clear the pathways and channels long damaged in my own thinking, which still, from time to time, produce unwanted horrors and streams of thought that are painful to navigate.

I was driving one day asking the Power that I believe in to give me a means and an idea to correct my own thinking somehow, one that lay outside the realms of pharmaceutical intervention and heavy medical imaging of injecting dyes and scanning for patterns and results. It was perhaps a day later when a simple but comforting image came to me: the image was my head surrounded by a group of small hummingbirds in flight. Iridescent yet without form, I could hear the flicker of their tiny wings beating madly about as they would circle my head. I could feel — *literally feel* — a gentle poke from their narrow beaks as they would re-harness and sew together damaged or lost connections, pecking away at old neural pathways that lay long dead, tying together the strands of nervous tissue regarded for mental health. Every morning, for weeks and months, the same visual would come to me. I would sit, quietly sipping coffee as a track with chimes and bells would draw me into a relaxed state, while the simple and effective imagery of my head surrounded with birds would unfold. They would peck away, correcting and sewing, like small creatures making a neat and tidy nest fit for bearing new life. After fifteen or twenty minutes, I would let the image fall away finish my coffee, and go about my work for the day. It was this — I can say with some finality — that silenced decades of old ruptures in my psyche, where the darkest parts of my soul used to live.

ABOUT THE AUTHOR

Jeff Gould is an author, blogger, humorist, and public speaker who has worked in the field of addiction and substance abuse as a crisis interventionist/program administrator for over a decade. He has been very active as a champion for the homeless, with an avocational history working in global disaster response. Jeff lives a modest and quiet life in Dallas Texas, and enjoys spending time writing, or playing music at home with his wife Hilary and their three cats.